DATE DUE

DEMCO 38-296

Georgine N. Olson
Editor

Fiction Acquisition/ Fiction Management: Education and Training

Fiction Acquisition/Fiction Management: Education and Training has been co-published simultaneously as *The Acquisitions Librarian,* Number 19 1998.

Pre-publication REVIEWS, COMMENTARIES, EVALUATIONS . . .

"**F**iction Acquisition/Fiction Management: Education and Training is a new addition to a relatively small amount of literature on the subject. Olson has long been an advocate, and she repeats some basic points here (e.g., the need for public libraries to devote resources to reference and readers' advisory tools that are helpful in acquiring, developing, and promoting fiction collections suited to the desires and wants of community residents; and the critical need for more education–both by grassroots groups such as the Adult Readers' Round Table in the Chicago area and the nation's schools of library and information science)."

Sharon L. Baker, PhD
Associate Professor
University of Iowa
School of Library and Information Science

Fiction Acquisition/ Fiction Management: Education and Training

Fiction Acquisition/Fiction Management: Education and Training has been co-published simultaneously as *The Acquisitions Librarian*, Number 19 1998.

These books were published simultaneously as special thematic issues of *The Acquisitions Librarian* and are available bound separately. Visit Haworth's website at http://www.haworth.com to search our online catalog for complete tables of contents and ordering information for these and other publications. Or call 1-800-HAWORTH (outside US/Canada: 607-722-5857), Fax: 1-800-895-0582 (outside US/Canada: 607-771-0012), or e-mail getinfo@ haworth.com

Fiction Acquisition/ Fiction Management: Education and Training

Georgine N. Olson
Editor

Fiction Acquisition/Fiction Management: Education and Training has been co-published simultaneously as *The Acquisitions Librarian*, Number 19 1998.

The Haworth Press, Inc.
New York • London

Fiction Acquisition/Fiction Management: Education and Train-ing has been co-published simultaneously as *The Acquisitions Librarian*, Number 19 1998.

Cover design by Thomas J. Mayshock Jr.

The Haworth Press, Inc., 10 Alice Street, Binghamton, NY 13904-1580 USA

Library of Congress Cataloging-in-Publication Data

Fiction acquisition/fiction management : education and training / Georgine N. Olson, editor.
    p. cm.
    "Fiction acquisition/fiction management : education and training, has been co-published si-multaneously as The Acquisitions Librarian, number 19, 1998."
    Includes bibliographical references and index.
    ISBN 0-7890-0391-0
    1. Fiction in libraries–United States. I. Olson, Georgine N.

Z711.5.F53 1998
025.2'780883–dc21   97-49336
                                                                                                        CIP

INDEXING & ABSTRACTING

Contributions to this publication are selectively indexed or abstracted in print, electronic, online, or CD-ROM version(s) of the reference tools and information services listed below. This list is current as of the copyright date of this publication. See the end of this section for additional notes.

- *Central Library & Documentation Bureau,* International Labour Office, CH-1211 Geneva 22, Switzerland

- *CNPIEC Reference Guide: Chinese National Directory of Foreign Periodicals,* P.O. Box 88, Beijing, People's Republic of China

- *Combined Health Information Database (CHID),* National Institutes of Health, 3 Information Way, Bethesda, MD 20892-3580

- *Current Awareness Abstracts,* Association for Information Management, Information House, 20-24 Old Street, London, EC1V 9AP, England

- *Educational Administration Abstracts (EAA),* Sage Publications, Inc., 2455 Teller Road, Newbury Park, CA 91320

- *IBZ International Bibliography of Periodical Literature,* Zeller Verlag GmbH & Co., P.O. Box 1949, d-49009 Osnabruck, Germany

- *Index to Periodical Articles Related to Law,* University of Texas, 727 East 26th Street, Austin, TX 78705

- *Information Reports & Bibliographies,* Science Associates International, Inc., 6 Hastings Road, Marlboro, NJ 07746-1313

- *Information Science Abstracts,* Plenum Publishing Company, 233 Spring Street, New York, NY 10013-1578

- *Informed Librarian, The,* Infosources Publishing, 140 Norma Road, Teaneck, NJ 07666

- *INSPEC Information Services,* Institution of Electrical Engineers, Michael Faraday House, Six Hills Way, Stevenage, Herts SG1 2AY, England

(continued)

- *INTERNET ACCESS (& additional networks) Bulletin Board for Libraries ("BUBL"), coverage of information resources on INTERNET, JANET, and other networks.*
  - <URL:http://bubl.ac.uk/>
  - The new locations will be found under <URL:http://bubl.ac.uk/link/>.
  - Any existing BUBL users who have problems finding information on the new service should contact the BUBL help line by sending e-mail to <bubl@bubl.ac.uk>. The Andersonian Library, Curran Building, 101 St. James Road, Glasgow G4 0NS, Scotland

- *Journal of Academic Librarianship: Guide to Professional Literature, The,* Graduate School of Library & Information Science/Simmons College, 300 The Fenway, Boston, MA 02115-5898

- *Library & Information Science Abstracts (LISA),* Bowker-Saur Limited, Maypole House, Maypole Road, East Grinstead, West Sussex RH19 1HH, England

- *Library Literature,* The H.W. Wilson Company, 950 University Avenue, Bronx, NY 10452

- *National Clearinghouse on Child Abuse & Neglect,* 10530 Rosehaven Street, Suite 400, Fairfax, VA 22030-2804

- *Newsletter of Library and Information Services,* China Sci-Tech Book Review, Library of Academia Sinica, 8 Kexueyuan Nanlu, Zhongguancun, Beijing 100080, People's Republic of China

- *NIAAA Alcohol and Alcohol Problems Science Database (ETOH)*, National Institute on Alcohol Abuse and Alcoholism, 1400 Eye Street NW, Suite 600, Washington, DC 20005

- *PASCAL,* % Institute de L'Information Scientifique et Technique. Cross-disciplinary electronic database covering the fields of science, technology & medicine. Also available on CD-ROM, and can generate customized retrospective searches. For more information: INIST, Customer Desk, 2, allee du Parc de Brabois, F-54514 Vandoeuvre Cedex, France; (http//www.inist.fr), INIST/CNRS-Service Gestion des Documents Primaires, 2, allee du Parc de Brabois, F-54514 Vandoeuvre-les-Nancy, Cedex, France

- *REHABDATA, National Rehabilitation Information Center (NARIC),* 8455 Colesville Road, Suite 935, Silver Spring, MD 20910-3319

(continued)

SPECIAL BIBLIOGRAPHIC NOTES

related to special journal issues (separates)
and indexing/abstracting

☐ indexing/abstracting services in this list will also cover material in any "separate" that is co-published simultaneously with Haworth's special thematic journal issue or DocuSerial. Indexing/abstracting usually covers material at the article/chapter level.

☐ monographic co-editions are intended for either non-subscribers or libraries which intend to purchase a second copy for their circulating collections.

☐ monographic co-editions are reported to all jobbers/wholesalers/approval plans. The source journal is listed as the "series" to assist the prevention of duplicate purchasing in the same manner utilized for books-in-series.

☐ to facilitate user/access services all indexing/abstracting services are encouraged to utilize the co-indexing entry note indicated at the bottom of the first page of each article/chapter/contribution.

☐ this is intended to assist a library user of any reference tool (whether print, electronic, online, or CD-ROM) to locate the monographic version if the library has purchased this version but not a subscription to the source journal.

☐ individual articles/chapters in any Haworth publication are also available through the Haworth Document Delivery Service (HDDS).

Fiction Acquisition/ Fiction Management: Education and Training

CONTENTS

ABOUT THE EDITOR

Georgine N. Olson, MLS, is Outreach Services Manager of the Fairbanks North Star Borough Public Library and Regional Center in Fairbanks, Alaska. She has held various consulting and coordinating positions with Illinois library systems and served as Chair of the Association of Specialized and Cooperative Agencies' Cooperative Collection Development Discussion Group from 1993 to 1995. Olson is co-editor of and contributor to the book *Cooperative Collection Management: The Conspectus Approach* (1994), and editor of *Illinois Libraries: Reference Services in Illinois Libraries* (1991). She is presently a member of the Public Library Association Adult Lifelong Learning Section Committee.

Fiction Acquisition/Fiction Management: Education and Training

Georgine N. Olson

SUMMARY. This article discusses the need for education and training of librarians in the skills necessary to successful fiction acquisition and fiction collection management. It reviews some of the means used to determine what kinds of training are needed and what methods of delivery seem to be most effective in delivering this type of professional education. *[Article copies available for a fee from The Haworth Document Delivery Service: 1-800-342-9678. E-mail address: getinfo@haworth.com]*

What is it about fiction in libraries, anyhow?

Once we start referring to a body of material as "fiction" instead of "literature," strange things begin to happen to otherwise perfectly normal collection management processes–and the librarians behind those processes.

In most public libraries, fiction accounts for 50% or more of the total circulation. Yet, do we devote anywhere near that percentage to the training of fiction selectors–or to the reference tools that would be helpful in the acquisition and development of a fiction collection suited to the needs of the library user, consistent with the library's mission, plan of service, and collection development plan? Of course not!

Georgine N. Olson is Outreach Services Manager, Fairbanks North Star Borough Public Library and Regional System, 1215 Cowles Street, Fairbanks, AK 99701.

[Haworth co-indexing entry note]: "Fiction Acquisition/Fiction Management: Education and Training." Olson, Georgine N. Co-published simultaneously in *The Acquisitions Librarian* (The Haworth Press, Inc.) No. 19, 1998, pp. 1-9; and: *Fiction Acquisition/Fiction Management: Education and Training* (ed: Georgine N. Olson) The Haworth Press, Inc., 1998, pp. 1-9. Single or multiple copies of this article are available for a fee from The Haworth Document Delivery Service [1-800-342-9678, 9:00 a.m. - 5:00 p.m. (EST)]. E-mail address: getinfo@haworth.com].

FICTION_L: DISCUSSION ON THE INTERNET

A few short months of participating in *fiction_l*, a readers' advisory listserve (contact address: fiction_l@listserv.nslsilus.org), shows both a crying need for training–and a wonderful breadth of readily shared knowledge. Queries posted this spring included requests for:

Guidelines to weeding large print collections;

Sources for books on CD (discussion ensued as to their usefulness);

Suggestions of titles for a new classics list (published in the last 15 years);

Titles useful in genre fiction collection development.

Relatively new to the list and mulling over facets of fiction collection management, I posted the following:

Just how do we train librarians in the selection and development of popular materials collections, especially fiction?

. . . . How and where do we all develop the skills to build a collection that meets the (known/perceived) needs of our patrons in the most cost effective manner possible?

Going beyond books–how do we develop those skills, that knowledge to insure that our popular video and books-on-tape collections meet sound collection management criteria?

And–if it's not learned in academic settings, when and how do librarians either with or without a master's degree learn this . . . ?

I happen to think that–particularly in a time of diminishing resources and increasing demand–we need to insure that librarians not only know what we're doing, but also be able to prove/demonstrate this capability to administrators and governing bodies.

Over the next few days there was quite a bit of discussion, much of it keyed to the reader's advisory aspect of the question, but several people posted comments germane to the collection management aspects.

–"Have reader's advisory reference sources."–That is, build a fiction readers reference collection.

–"People coming out of library school don't have the background in books that reader's advisory calls for." An observation which would be just as valid for fiction selectors and collection development officers.

—"Library schools should acquaint their students with the review sources and give them a budget to spend for a described clientele."

—"Make it known to library schools that their graduates are unacceptable . . . A school which cannot place graduates in jobs is not long for this world."

—"Has anybody ever written to ALA's Committee on Accreditation about this?"

—"We can't let the mainstay of libraries, the fiction reader, to be left floundering around looking for a good book. They will go elsewhere, like bookstores, to get their help." If we don't build a collection to meet user's needs, they will "vote with their feet." Libraries lose without even knowing that there was a contest.

—"Staff members would meet once a month to discuss a particular genre . . . We published annotated bibliographies and keep them in a notebook which we used to jog our memories . . . " Including selectors and public services staff in these meetings would increase fiction skills for both groups.

—"RA (reader's advisory) is a very hands-on skill. I hope library schools can teach this, but I'm not sure how. It's like selection; we can teach them what tools to use, but we can't teach them what to select."

—"I think a course could be developed. Students wouldn't walk out as experts but at least they would have a general base of knowledge from which to work. The RA workshops at PLA, for example, contained more info than was available in lib. ed. courses."

—"Both the development of selection techniques and the training of readers advisory librarians in a small setting is really flying by the seat of our pants." Resources to help the practicing librarian need to be developed and made readily available.

—"One of the most distressing issues . . . is how selection and development of the fiction collection has been taken out of the hands of the librarian/selector . . .

leasing multiple copies . . .

buy every BOMC or Lit Guild book selection . . .

and every title that makes most of the standard best seller lists . . .

any fiction title in a series that we support . . .

any fiction title that generates large publicity campaigns or has a huge print run . . .

throw in Oprah and the paperback reprints . . .

there is virtually nothing left for the librarian to decide–we are out of money.

no funds for new authors, experimental fiction, foreign fiction, or short story collections . . . "

SURVEYING SMALL AND MEDIUM-SIZED LIBRARIES

In January 1992 the Collection Development and Evaluation Section (CODES) of the then named Reference and Adult Services Division (RASD) of the American Library Association (ALA) established an ad hoc committee on small and medium-sized libraries. The charge to this committee was to "Determine what collection management resources are available for librarians in small and medium-sized libraries of all types: investigate options for RASD/CODES." I was one of the members of that committee.

A committee member's review of the literature revealed very little in the way of current publications of use to this group of libraries.

Surveys distributed to state libraries and regional association chapters found that 72% of the 37 state libraries responding and 62% of the 42 chapters *had* provided programs on collection development for small and medium-sized libraries in the last five years. We also learned that 70% of the state libraries and 44% of the association chapters *planned* to provide more of the same in the near future. Eighty-six percent of the chapters and 75% of the state libraries indicated that they would welcome assistance from RASD/CODES in serving the collection development needs of these libraries. When it came to specifics, the state libraries leaned toward preferring RASD/CODES prepared handbooks or manuals, while the chapters indicated strong preference for packaged presentations for conferences and meetings.

My assignment was to develop a survey soliciting input from those in charge of collection management in small and medium-sized libraries, which, for the purposes of this survey, meant staffs of 1 to 25 librarians. Unable to secure funding for systematic distribution of the survey, we found interested librarians at the Public Library Association March 1993 Chicago workshops (one was devoted to collection management), the Illinois Library Association Conference in April 1993, and at the California Association's meeting in May 1993. The Illinois State Library facilitated distribution of the survey to the state's public libraries. Complete responses were returned from 43 libraries (including one academic library) in seven states.

Twenty-five of the libraries served communities with a population of 20,000 or less; 16 served fewer than 10,000.

Thirty-two of the respondents regularly read *Library Journal* and 23 regularly read *Booklist*. A frequent comment was that the special bibliographies in those journals were particularly helpful for collection development.

Twenty-three search professional literature for information on collection management issues; 13 rely on staff of regional systems; 9 rely on their peers.

When asked about the value of continuing education workshops, 20 indicated that they attend less than three continuing education workshops in a year. Most wanted local or regional workshops; only 11 would travel over 100 miles to attend a workshop. A clear majority of 27 preferred compact all-day CE, but 14 were amenable to attending a series of more detailed half-day sessions (if they weren't too far away). Although 27 indicated that the library budgeted for CE, only 13 were sure they could afford $100 for a CE program, but 30 were pretty sure they could afford about $50. Sixteen found the idea of CEUs appealing (3 asked what a CEU was). Eighteen had access to video conferencing downlink sites; 27 were interested in self-paced educational tools.

Even if you have just skimmed the numbers above, you probably noticed that the resources and training that interest the libraries differ significantly from those the state libraries and association chapters provide or plan to provide . . .

For 20, the sponsor or source of the program was important. A whopping 35 were more likely to seek out CE at a local or regional program rather than at an ALA Conference. This has tremendous ramifications for the RASD/CODES potential response to the Ad Hoc Committee's final report. In fact, the committee's top recommendation was that CODES should publish a series of short "how to" articles in the journals read by librarians in small and medium-sized libraries (*LJ* and/or *Booklist*). The second primary suggestion was that CODES should create workshop materials and train trainers for state and regional programs for librarians in small and medium-sized libraries. In both instances, fiction was one of the ten main topics to be addressed. Thus far, no action has been taken on any of these recommendations.

ARRT: STUNNED BY THE OBVIOUS?

Perhaps the library responses to the RASD/CODES ad hoc committee survey helps explain the history of the Chicago area Adult Reading Round Table (ARRT), a local organization devoted to readers' advisory services. Founded in 1985, their first day-long genre fiction workshop, gutsily presented a scant year later, drew 120 information-hungry librarians.

Programs presented by ARRT, and some of its "offspring" like MI-RAGe (Mid Illinois Readers Advisory Group) consistently (over)fill their venues. It seems to make little difference whether the program is genre-related or a librarian's how-to on some aspect of collection management or marketing. When presented regionally, the programs are usually half a day, with a full-day program every now and then. On a simple cost-recovery basis, using local expertise, most half-day programs, including meals and bountiful pertinent handouts and bibliographies, cost those attending less than $50.

Also, a search for recent publications related to fiction management and readers' services will show that early members of ARRT's steering committee (Ted Balcom, Merle Jacob, Georgine Olson, Joyce Saricks) have a sizeable number of citations among them for books and articles dealing with managing fiction collections, genre fiction, and various aspects of reader services. Is it that this group of people is so outstanding–or is it rather that they have developed a knowledge and expertise that meets the very real need of working librarians and has been sadly lacking in professional literature?

These programs and publications are bringing to fiction collection management just what the librarians indicated they wanted in their responses to the above-mentioned RASD/CODES committee survey.

WHAT ABOUT TRAINING NEW PROFESSIONALS?

One of this spring's discussions on fiction_l concerned training of reader's advisors, a.k.a. fiction specialists. Ricki Nordmeyer, an ARRT member and Reader's Advisory Specialist at Skokie Public Library, wrote that ARRT recently sent letters to all library schools in the United States emphasizing the need for coursework in reader's advisory services, which of course would include the study of popular materials, i.e., genre fiction. The few institutions responding felt they were addressing that need and declined ARRT's offer to help develop such a curriculum.

However, Dominican University is adding an experimental course in Reader's Advisory. In fact, Bill Crowley, who will be teaching the course, posted this notice on the internet on May 13, 1997:

> Dominican University (formerly Rosary College) is seeking up to a dozen volunteers to help design a revived Reader's Advisory Course within its Graduate School of Library and Information Science.

Crowley indicated that a version of this course is now being taught as part of their program at the College of St. Catherine in Minnesota. He also indicated that, after a one semester trial, faculty will vote on whether a reader's advisory course should be added to the permanent GSLIS curriculum.

I'd like to share a quote from Crowley's May 13 fiction_l posting that is in itself a very strong justification for better reader's advisory (and fiction collection development) training:

> I volunteered to teach this course because I . . . know that fiction readers are second only to genealogists in their willingness to commit mayhem in support of good public library programs.

WHAT ABOUT NON-PROFESSIONALS?

Many of our smaller public libraries are run by staff with no formal training in library science. Like a worker trying to live on minimum wage, these libraries and their staffs face challenges in making ends meet while delivering primary library service to their communities that boggle the mind. If the library's *entire* annual budget is $20,000, $5,000 for library materials is exceedingly generous. But, just how much can that $5,000 buy–and–how critically important is it that the materials purchased are *exactly* what the library's users need?

Burns Davis of the Nebraska Library Commission has worked closely with several of the state's small libraries (which happen to be just about *all* of the libraries in the state) to train the librarians in use of conspectus-based assessment of their collections, including fiction collections. By bringing into consideration the age and use of the collection and by showing libraries how they can tailor formal assessment tools to meet local needs, librarians are not only learning how to use sophisticated management tools, they are putting this knowledge to practical use in better meeting the needs of their patrons.

In 1991, two central Illinois library systems worked with the University of Iowa's Sharon Baker on an LSCA funded project to develop tools that would enable librarians in small libraries (serving populations of less than 10,000) to more effectively manage fiction collections. Ten libraries participated; four face-to-face half-day meetings were held during the grant year and each participating library tested two of the group of management tools developed for the project. In 1992, Lincoln Trail Libraries System in Champaign, Illinois, published the *Fiction Collection Assessment Manual*, which includes all of the instruments the librarians tested.

As one of the two system consultants working with the project, I watched the participating librarians grow in confidence and professionalism as the year progressed–and beyond. Libraries that couldn't afford to automate their collections found the means to become participants in their system's regional database. Librarians who were self-effacing to the point of invisibility began to speak up at board meetings and guide their boards to more proactive library service. Librarians whose previous job experience had been limited to clerking in a local shop worked with the development and implementation of fairly sophisticated cooperative collection management programs involving various aspects of fiction collection development and resource sharing.

To be honest, it was *not* the tools we developed that caused these changes. It was the realization that there were resources that could help a library do a better job–and that staff *could* learn how to use them whether or not they were "real" librarians. It was those face-to-face meetings where they could discuss common problems with their peers–and learn how these problems could be handled. It was the availability of consultants and experts in the field–and the realization that these people were there to work *with* everyone involved.

Both the Nebraska and Illinois experiences are concrete examples that reinforce what the RASD/CODES ad hoc committee learned about how small and medium-sized libraries feel they can participate in and learn more about collection development and evaluation.

WHERE DO WE GO FROM HERE?

It would appear that we are moving forward in professionalizing the popular fiction/reader's advisory field. Since many a library selected Popular Reading Materials Center as one of its primary roles when participating in planning and role setting exercises–and successful popular reading materials collections are inherently patron-responsive–it is not unlikely that the profession will see changes in the acquisition and management of popular materials collections, which, of course, are largely fiction collections. And–it's about time that we do so!

Providing the Fiction Your Patrons Want: Managing Fiction in a Medium-Sized Public Library

Joyce G. Saricks

SUMMARY. This article offers practical advice on fiction selection and collection management and underlines the importance of flexibility and common sense in establishing acquisitions guidelines and procedures. In the first section, which emphasizes the actual selection and acquisition of fiction, there are tips to assist selectors, advice on setting up a budget, and suggestions for collection development and weeding. In the second part, which focuses on methods to use in working with patrons and staff to use the materials, there are suggestions of straightforward and reasonably simple techniques that can highlight fiction collections and aid in their use. Throughout, emphasis is placed on the importance of understanding what an individual library's readers need, both for leisure reading and more serious pursuits, as well as on the necessity of involving all staff and patrons in the acquisitions process. *[Article copies available for a fee from The Haworth Document Delivery Service: 1-800-342-9678. E-mail address: getinfo@haworth.com]*

If there was a course in Acquisitions at my library school, I didn't take it. And even if I had taken such a course, I'm certain it could not have been as useful as twenty years' direct experience as a selector in a busy me-

Joyce G. Saricks is Literature and Audio Services Coordinator, Downers Grove Public Library, 1050 Curtiss, Downers Grove, IL 60515.

[Haworth co-indexing entry note]: "Providing the Fiction Your Patrons Want: Managing Fiction in a Medium-Sized Public Library." Saricks, Joyce G. Co-published simultaneously in *The Acquisitions Librarian* (The Haworth Press, Inc.) No. 19, 1998, pp. 11-28; and: *Fiction Acquisition/Fiction Management: Education and Training* (ed: Georgine N. Olson) The Haworth Press, Inc., 1998, pp. 11-28. Single or multiple copies of this article are available for a fee from The Haworth Document Delivery Service [1-800-342-9678, 9:00 a.m. - 5:00 p.m. (EST)]. E-mail address: getinfo@haworth.com].

dium-sized public library. While courses may teach basics, they usually don't address the subtler issues involved in creating and carrying out a selection plan that meets the diverse needs of the community that uses a particular library. Through experience–talking with patrons, watching reserve and best sellers lists–and much trial and error, librarians, especially those who select fiction, gain that intuitive sense of the kinds of books their patrons seek. In order to elucidate this process beyond the basics one might expect to learn in library school, I want to focus on two aspects of fiction acquisition: first, the actual selection and acquisition of materials (including budgeting, collection development, and weeding), and secondly, methods of working with patrons and staff to use these materials, since that is, after all, the point of acquisitions.

SELECTION AND ACQUISITIONS

Selection Tips

First, I want to share some suggestions that may streamline selection and acquisitions. These techniques make us better selectors and cover aspects of acquisitions most of us didn't learn in library school but have certainly come to recognize in the real world of public libraries.

Selectors Should Work the Desk

In my experience, the best selection is done by staff who interact with library users on a regular basis. Popular materials collections should by their nature reflect what's most in demand at a particular library. Not what reviewers and publishers say is or should be popular, but what your readers want to read. Discovering what's popular can be done most easily while working the desk; it requires more initiative on the part of the selector not regularly scheduled to work with readers.

Selectors who also have desk responsibilities know the kinds of books readers request, and what they find–or don't find–on the shelves. If we work the desk, we go to the shelves regularly; we see what's there, including titles or types of books that *never* seem to be checked out, and we learn quickly what specific titles or authors or genres we never seem to have enough of. For example, knowing John Grisham is immensely popular is not the same as facing readers, day in and day out, who despair because they've read all Grisham's books and need someone else "just like" him. Placed in this situation, we scour the journals, seeking other authors who might work for these readers. We're conscious of a need and work to fill it; we're invested in finding a solution, because we know how frequently we face this question. When we work on the desk and interact with readers, we gain a solid background in the kinds of fiction popular at our libraries, and we then apply this knowledge to our book selection.

It's not always possible for all selectors to work the desk. However, selectors who don't need to develop ways to ensure that they get this feedback and develop this background. If you are a selector who doesn't work the desk, you need to make a special effort to know what's being talked about, in addition to what's checked out and reserved. There are several techniques which can help these selectors (not to mention the rest of us who do work the desk). Keeping a list of all authors, titles, and genres patrons ask for and indicating those requests that can't be filled can be useful, even if it's only kept for short periods. Querying librarians who do work the desk, asking them about trends and collection deficiencies, is always helpful. They can keep you up-to-date on hot authors, genres, and subgenres in your library. Talking with shelvers, especially if they are assigned specific areas to shelve, can also be very revealing. If anyone knows what has been checked out and returned, they do.

Active listening and monitoring of patron requests are important for all selectors, whether they work the desk or not. An additional benefit of these practices is that we become aware of patron issues beyond selection and gain expertise in providing service with the collection. For example, a request for assistance finding an author may lead to a discussion of separating out genre collections so patrons can more easily find what they are looking for. Or several queries on a topic may indicate the need for a display or a booklist. Selection of materials should not be done in a vacuum; good selectors see the implications of all their interactions. Stressing the importance of an awareness of reading tastes and trends makes all staff aware of *listening* to what patrons talk about and request.

Actively Solicit Suggestions for Purchase from Readers, Both Library Patrons and Staff

Although my experience is with autonomous, independent selectors rather than a selection committee, I don't want to give the impression that we work in isolation. In addition to reading reviews, we take suggestions from both patrons and staff. For example, we encourage patrons to fill out a reserve card as a suggestion, if a book doesn't already show "on order" on the computer. We can guarantee a popular author's books will be ordered, as soon as we have enough information to do so, and that others will be considered for purchase–and we do buy a number of books just because patrons request them, even if the reviews don't warrant purchase. If we don't purchase a title, often because it's not available, we will obtain it through inter-library loan. (And if we're getting a lot of inter-library loan requests for a particular author or genre, we know this is something we should add and/or an area to consider for collection development.)

All staff are encouraged to read all reviews, whether they select that area or not, and either fill out staff reserves as suggestions or make comments by the reviews in the journals. We need to take staff suggestions seriously, particularly since we're trained to observe trends in popular authors and genres and may have reason to believe a book will be a good addition to the collection.

Even though certain staff may be assigned selection responsibilities for specific areas, I believe better selection is done–and better service provided–when all public service staff are encouraged to participate in the book acquisition process, either by reading reviews and actually selecting titles for purchase or by providing suggestions to selectors. No one person, nor even a group of staff, can really know enough to make all the right choices. When all staff feel empowered to suggest, and suggestions are solicited from patrons as well, a well-balanced collection is more likely to be the result.

Reviews Don't Tell the Whole Story, and They Can't Be the Entire Source of Titles in Book Selection

Most of the selections we make are based on reviews from a wide range of professional and popular sources. At my library we always try to buy from reviews, unless we are ordering an author who is already popular in our library. If you've ever survived a serious materials challenge, you probably rely heavily on reviews, too!

Book selection, the foundation of all our collection development, is a complicated task. Not only might we find as many varying opinions as journals in which a title is reviewed, we must also come to recognize what to look for when we read reviews. At least one standard journal which we read faithfully seems to pan almost everything–and the titles it praises seem far too esoteric for my clientele. Another journal provides only positive reviews. Does that mean everything it covers would fit my collection? Of course not. We need to learn how to recognize their biases and how to use both types of journals and everything in between, to learn to read reviews for the clues as to a title's suitability to our readers. Again, this implies that we have a good sense of what our readers enjoy: what they request and what they read. We must also recognize that tastes and audiences change. As a result we'll occasionally try an interesting-sound-ing title outside the perceived profile of our reading public's interests. It's important, if we can afford to do so, to buy well-reviewed books outside the mainstream. Although we work to know what our readers like, there is also often a non-vocal readership for authors, titles, and types of books, a minority audience who may enjoy those esoteric or "literary" titles, for example. We should try to discover these readers and offer a range of titles beyond what's popular to satisfy this audience.

Selection from reviews is an inexact science at best. Reviews of the same title may differ widely from journal to journal, and even when a book is highly praised, there is no guarantee it will find an audience in our libraries, while a book that's bashed may have a reserve queue that will take months to fill. A review is one reader's impression, how a title affected him or her on a particular day. Staff need to learn to apply reviews to what they know about what is popular at your library.

As an aside, it's interesting to note that more and more reviews are acknowledging similar authors, comparing lesser-known authors to more popular ones or placing authors within a popular genre or subgenre. Because reviewers understand the value of such comparisons to public service librarians, they often draw on their reading experience and add comments along the lines of "for fans of Mary Higgins Clark," or "with the pacing of Grisham and the characterizations of LeCarre." These comments in reviews help us see the potential audience for the title in our libraries and buy accordingly. (I do, however, advise checking out such comments by at least skimming some of these books. Because that is not always possible, when I share this comment with readers, I say that reviewers, rather than I, have made this connection. Then I ask them to let me know if they agree.)

Remember, also, that professional journals should not be our only source of reviews. Also in demand are book club selections as well as titles covered in other media: local newspapers, popular magazines, television, and radio. It behooves us to check these sources as well, so we can be prepared for requests. We don't often find ourselves asked for a title, reviewed in these media, that has completely escaped our notice, but if we're checking the same sources our reading public uses to learn about new titles, we're better prepared for their requests.

Be Adventurous and Creative in Dividing Selection Responsibilities

Selecting and collection development for the entire fiction collection can be an overwhelming responsibility. However, many of us feel saddled with this responsibility, because it seems difficult to divide the collection reasonably. Non-fiction division, by Dewey number or LC classification, seems so much more straightforward. When I broached this problem with my administrator, he provided me with a solution so simple it's almost frightening: We simply divided the fiction selection responsibilities in half. One person buys all books by authors A-L, the other, M-Z. (For some reason, there seem to be more reviews earlier in the alphabet, hence, the uneven division.). One could probably divide the collection into thirds, or even fourths. We divide Mystery selection responsibilities in the same way, and may divide Science Fiction/Fantasy in the next few years. Under this arrangement, each of us has a clear alphabetic selection area, without overlap (except in cases for which the genre classification is unclear, but we have those problems in any case, no matter how selection is done); in fact, we probably have fewer problems deciding who buys what than do some non-fiction selectors. (For example, will that new psychology book go in 150, Psychology, or 616, Psychiatry? It's often hard to tell from reviews, and sometimes both the selector in the 100s and the 600s will purchase.) In addition, rather than having a separate selector for paperbacks, the same selectors choose paperbacks in their alphabetical sections. They have a better sense of what they have bought in hardcover and what was popular, so they can more accurately and efficiently select paperbacks.

If you don't now, consider changing selection responsibilities on a regular basis. We change ours every other year. That gives us enough time to become familiar with a section and become comfortable selecting. Changing adds variety to our job and keeps us from becoming stale. It combats any biases selectors might have, and it expands what each of us knows about the entire collection and the reviews. As we work through the new areas, we gain confidence in larger and larger parts of the collection and thus serve patrons better.

Selection Procedures Should Lead to Timely and Efficient Acquisition of Materials

Because I've always worked in a situation in which selectors operate fairly autonomously, selecting within assigned areas and budget, I'm biased toward that practice. It's difficult for me to imagine how a committee selects books as quickly, efficiently, and effectively. No matter how selection is done in your library, I believe it's important to acquire books as expeditiously as possible.

If patrons were asked the most important library function, many would say to get popular books quickly—into the library and into their hands. And if they see this as one of our prime responsibilities, we should, too. As soon as a reader hears about a title—or worse, sees it in a bookstore—he wonders where our copy is. Knowing it's on order or in processing assures readers we're taking their needs seriously, getting the book into their hands as quickly as possible.

We keep our journals at one desk and selectors read and initial titles they wish to order. When everyone has done this, the journal is sent to Technical Services for ordering, and they place orders weekly with job-bers. In fact, if one of our selectors has dawdled or been away, I may send the journal on and let that librarian order later.

Unfortunately, even if we select titles quickly, we can't guarantee when books will actually be acquired and processed. We have to rely on Techni-cal Services. Please excuse a small digression here into the pains and pleasures of inter-departmental cooperation. I have heard horror stories of Technical Services departments that literally rule the library, and they certainly have the power to do so. They can also make acquisitions, collec-tion development, and almost all aspects of our service to the public a true joy.

While other public service staff get all the credit for their hard work and fiction librarians have all the fun, no library can operate effectively with-out a really good Technical Services department. Since I've been there—worked as head of Technical Services–I know they get very little praise and myriad problems. I am lucky to work in a library that has the world's best Technical Services department, bar none, and I try never to pass up an opportunity to give them the credit they deserve. They work hard, quickly and efficiently ordering and processing materials. And they fix problems, recatalog materials, and generally make it possible for us to serve patrons better.

Technical Services can make public service staff's lives a misery or a joy. If your Technical Services staff doesn't know–or care–enough to process a really hot book as soon as it comes in, you've got a problem. If they don't order on a regular basis so that those popular titles appear shortly after readers see them in bookstores, you need to negotiate.

We're the "public" that Technical Services needs to deal with face to face, and we can be as disruptive as the worst problem patrons. But, as library staff, they need to work to serve their "public," whether it be public service departments directly or library users indirectly, to the best of their ability. And as that public, we need to be reasonable, sensible in our requests, and effusive in our thanks. (Brownies–for that matter, choco-late in any form–are a particularly useful currency in my library.) The relationship between Technical and Public Services staff shouldn't be that of parent and recalcitrant teenager (and I won't say which is which). Between us, we set up guidelines and follow them. We submit journals on a regular basis, and they send our orders regularly, at a set time. I know if I come in with a stack of journals at noon Tuesday, I'm waiting until next week for those titles to be ordered. On the other hand, if we're in desperate need of a really popular title, they may have enough orders to place an extra order, or they'll call the nearby bookstore and purchase the title there. (We don't do this often but there have been times when a title didn't get ordered or has been backordered. Knowing we can simply go out and buy a title has made a real difference in the level of service we provide.) They know this is important, and that I wouldn't ask if it weren't. Just as they understand the importance of some things to us–like having copies of best sellers as soon as they arrive–we try to be sensitive to their busy times and not create tasks that really aren't necessary.

Write Selection Guidelines Which Reflect the Library's Mission Statement

Especially if selectors operate independently, they need a sense of the scope of the collection and how to buy in order to meet set goals. To do this selectors need to know and understand the library's mission statement and the selection guidelines that have been created to help achieve the library's mission. However you structure your selection policy and guidelines, consider developing a policy that emphasizes the kind of collection you believe it is important to provide but which also allows for flexibility and professional decisions in achieving collection goals.

The mission statement of the Downers Grove Public Library charges selectors with providing "books, other materials, and services to meet users' needs for timely, accurate, and useful information,"[1] and stresses providing current, high-demand, and high-interest materials. Then we have four pages of "Selection Criteria," which cover, in some detail, considerations such as "Authority of Author," "Currency of Material," "Curriculum Support," "Local Interest," and "Popularity."[2] Unofficially, we also have guidelines to help us. For example, we buy all fiction on the *New York Times* and *Chicago Tribune* hardcover Best Sellers lists. We buy all books in series, no matter what the review. (Readers expect to read all the titles in a series and will forgive an occasional weak entry. When it's clear they're no longer reading a particular series, we may stop if reviews continue to be bad. However, we also spend considerable time and money filling in titles in series that we didn't purchase or no longer own, if the author and series become popular.) When the new title by a formerly popular author doesn't circulate and extra copies fill a shelf, we know we should buy fewer copies next time. It's also important to consider book club selections, books with enormous advertising budgets, and award winners. The first two will likely be requested, and the last probably should be owned.

If selectors have guidelines for what to buy initially, they also benefit from suggestions about multiple copies. Although our policy states that we buy multiple copies of materials in high demand, our practice of buying one extra copy for every five reserves is not part of policy. Even if it's a book we dislike, know is ephemeral, and which received terrible reviews, we stick to this policy. We also have the discretion to buy extra copies even if there are not five reserves, if the situation warrants, as when a book *always* has two-three reserves and never appears on the shelf. Usually that's the sign of a word-of-mouth book that will remain popular long enough to justify the investment in extra copies.

The best book selection benefits from a system of guidelines that supports acquisition and flexibility on the part of the selectors. We may have achieved balance in our selection today, but tomorrow something may tip the scales, and we need to be ready to adjust our formula. Not that we throw everything to the wind but that we recognize and acknowledge that selection guidelines must remain fluid. If our goal is to provide patrons with what they want to read, as well as what they expect to find in a library, we need to be open to providing titles that are requested by readers, or to recatalog a title or series to better fit the kind of requests we receive.

Train Selectors in the Library's Policy and Procedures;
Then Trust Them

Fiction selectors don't spring wholly formed from Zeus' head like Minerva; they're developed, step by step, and they're not static creations. They change and grow in their perception of how the library's patrons best use the collections the library provides. The corollary of this point is that selectors make mistakes. We all make selection mistakes, whether we're operating autonomously or as part of a selection committee. We'll never be able to predict accurately the tastes of our patrons–and neither do authors, publishers, or reviews. Selection requires juggling priorities: multiple copies of best-sellers versus a range of award-winners or more literary titles that may not be as popular; book club selections (and especially Oprah's books) against the titles that get extraordinary reviews in journals and then may sit on our shelves. We make choices, sometimes incorrectly, but we eventually develop a feel for a balance that works with our readers and our collection.

Someday there will be a useful computer program that simulates book selection, collecting and evaluating all the factors we have to consider–albeit unconsciously–when we read reviews. Until that point, we learn by trial and error–and pray the errors aren't major and/or expensive.

Budgeting

Before we go any further we need to address the issue of money. For many of us it's difficult to find money for discretionary purchases, after buying the most popular titles, the best sellers, and the award winners. How do we handle this problem? How do we budget money for fiction collections?

The first step is to design an adequate budget that reflects the incredible, but not always acknowledged, popularity of the fiction collection in most libraries. There is no doubt some justification for the paranoia that many of us feel: Fiction librarians and collections don't always get respect from the profession and often not from our administrators. When we discuss funding the collection, we get more respect if we come armed with statistics, but we need to be sensible and shrewd in what we offer. For example, comparing my fiction circulation to total circulation isn't nearly as effective as pointing out that fiction circulation alone constitutes 49% of all adult book circulation. None of the Dewey hundreds or biography can make such a claim. (With as excellent and active a Junior Room as my library boasts, I'd be foolish to include the children's circulation figures in my comparison, and, frankly, adding the audio collection would make this an apples-to-oranges comparison.) Not that I would then argue for 49% of the adult book budget, but with such a high circulation percentage, it's harder to ignore the value and popularity of the fiction collection and deny it a fair share of funds.

The next piece of data to know is how much the books cost. I've never found the averages in professional literature accurate. We keep order slips for two months every year and calculate the cost per item in each collection. (For example, total amount spent on mysteries divided by the total number of volumes bought during the period.) This is not completely accurate either, but it better reflects our purchasing patterns and costs. I also monitor the number of volumes added in each fiction collection (Fiction, Mysteries, Science Fiction/Fantasy, Paperbacks) each month, so I can estimate how many volumes to budget for. Then, when I create my budget, I estimate the amount to be spent for each collection as follows: we'll buy X volumes in Fiction (or Mystery, or SF/Fantasy) at $Y/each (with each collection having a separate cost figure) for a total of $Z. Not only do I have a sensible amount of money to request, but selectors have an idea of approximately how many books they should be buying each month. This system isn't perfect–no one can predict a string of runaway best-sellers and the devastation they can wreak on any budget–but it gives me and my administrator a sense of plan and direction.

Budgeting for popular titles is a separate problem. If you don't already have a rental, Hot Picks, or similar collection of really popular titles, I would suggest you consider one. We began our Rental Collection in 1978, when we could not keep up with demand for Colleen McCullough's *The Thorn Birds*. No matter how many extra copies we bought, we seemed unable to reduce that reserve queue. Thus we established a separate collection–and budget line–for extra copies of really popular titles.

We have always charged for rentals–the first day is free, then 20 cents a day–and this collection is self-supporting; we take in as much money as we spend for titles. We have never contracted for a special rental plan; every time we calculated costs–human costs of bookkeeping, returns, etc.–we decided self-selection was more cost effective for us, but I would advise each library to analyze these tradeoffs, as I know many who are very happy with commercial rental plans.

Since its inception, our rental collection has always included copies of fiction on the *New York Times* Best Sellers lists. We used to purchase the top ten non-fiction titles as well, but learned early on that these simply did not circulate as rentals. Other purchases are at our own discretion. When I read reviews, I often think of a particular reader who uses our rental collection almost exclusively as his source of reading material and who exemplifies, in my mind, the reader for whom we have created this collection. If I think this is a book he will enjoy and thus one that will be a popular rental title–usually fast-paced suspense and/or action-oriented novels–I always buy rental, as well as circulating, copies. If a book has accumulated nine to ten reserves, I'll buy a rental. There are some exceptions. Mystery titles, except for the few that make the best sellers lists, don't circulate as well in the rental collection. Many of our Mystery readers simply do not use this collection. We do buy some non-fiction rentals, but only those with long reserve lists or a local interest.

With a rental collection, we buy fewer total copies of really popular titles. Many readers, especially those who read quickly, would rather exercise the option of renting a book than of waiting in line. And even if they keep it a week, they're only spending $1.20, a fraction of what the book would cost them. (We do a brisk business before the library closes for a holiday, since closed days are free days, and readers can almost always find time to escape into a book they've been wanting to read, no matter how busy they are with holiday preparations.) We weed the rental collection at least monthly, more frequently if we see three to four copies of a title just sitting there. Rental labels are removed and the transferred rentals fill the reserve queue or go directly to the new fiction shelves.

Collection Development and Weeding

In recent years a number of useful articles on these topics have appeared in the literature, and I don't want to duplicate their efforts. I do, however, want to acknowledge some basic principles. First, although I've spoken for the most part of the need to provide popular materials in fiction collections, I strongly believe that any quality fiction collection is much more than just best sellers. We are building collections for all times, not just for today. As selectors, we need to be aware of the implications of all we add and withdraw and of how these changes affect the total collection. Our job is to develop a collection that meets the reading needs of a range of users, of diverse ages and interests, and it behooves us to have as extensive and varied a collection as possible.

On the other hand, we can't have every title every user requests. As I wrote earlier, a pattern of requests for authors or genres we don't have may mean that we need to consider these areas for collection development. We may have had to withdraw a title and been unable to replace it in any format. (For years we have considered both paperback and large type editions acceptable additions to the fiction collection when regular hardcover titles are unavailable.) If that's the case, we can only provide access through inter-library loan. However, our goal must be to do our best to build and maintain an extensive and diverse collection.

To this end we must make some difficult decisions about what we keep and in what format we make a title available. Although space has been a serious problem in my library for the last few years, we do keep multiple copies of books in several categories: classics, titles read for school assignments, books by currently popular authors, first books in popular series. Otherwise I expect Fiction titles to average seven circulations each year; if they don't, they are candidates for weeding.

Format is a more controversial issue. For years paperbacks have been the bane of the library profession. However, I think it's time we stop penalizing patrons whose favorite authors are available only in that format. In my library paperbacks on the browsing racks are cataloged (PB/F, PB/M, etc.) and are retrievable through the computer catalog. This has been the situation for as long as I have worked here and seems logical. Why would you have a collection that you have no access to? The cost of adding them to the database must be far less than the staff time spent trying to find them, day after day, for patrons. Looking for uncataloged material, which may or may not be on the shelf, is exceedingly frustrating for both staff and patrons and the collection becomes less useful. Unfortunately, many administrators fail to calculate this on-going staff time when they decide not to put items in the database.

We also have a growing number of paperbacks that are cataloged (as Fiction, Mystery, and/or Science Fiction/Fantasy) and intershelved with hardcovers. Like many other librarians, we started this practice with Science Fiction and Fantasy books, which were often available only in paperback. When we realized they were part of popular series, we decided simply to catalog them and put them on the regular shelves with the other Science Fiction and Fantasy. In the Mystery collection, too, many popular authors and series were only available in paperback, so we bought them, and slowly but surely integrated them into the hardcover Mystery collection. Now, when a hardcover title is out of print, we gratefully buy the paperback and add it to the collection in place of the hardcover. I've been surprised at how long many of these paperbacks have survived–certainly as long as some hardcover titles published by companies that care little about their bindings.

Binding is an important aspect of collection development, as it allows us to keep titles that we might otherwise be unable to replace. And in any case, binding is less expensive than buying new copies of titles. We now use a company that laminates the paper jacket on the rebound book, and we–and patrons–have been pleased that we can keep the covers and revitalize the books. (Covers at our library are extremely important, and books without covers circulate less frequently, unless they are actually put in a reader's hands. One day I want to do a display, Great Books Without Covers; it just might work!)

Finally, a few words about weeding. Unlike our colleagues in charge of non-fiction, we can't weed by publication date. Although trends in popularity change, fiction doesn't usually become outdated. It might be easier if it did. When I last weeded our fiction collection, desperate to create some space, I was amazed at how active the collection is and at how few titles I could justify withdrawing, outside of extra copies of titles by authors who are no longer as popular. It was both an exhilarating and depressing experience. It was also educational: I discovered a few more titles for our avid romantic suspense readers, candidates for the "Worst Cover" award, and several authors I never realized were so popular. Weeding is necessary to keep the collection fresh and the act increases our knowledge of our collection, but it's so time-intensive that it really becomes an expensive undertaking.

ACQUISITIONS AND OUR READERS

Time and money spent developing an excellent fiction collection are lost if we don't make that collection accessible to readers. Again, there are sources of this information in the literature, but I do want to highlight a few techniques we have found particularly useful.

New Books Collections

First, we separate the newer books from older titles, creating smaller collections where patrons can easily browse. New books have a sticker, indicating the 14-day circulation period, on the pocket. When the book is moved to the regular, 21-day circulating collection, we simply remove or cover the sticker. Shelvers take care of the entire process. All our books are stamped with the date they are processed. Every month a shelver checks the 14-day collection, removing all books that have been in the collection 9-12 months, covering the stickers, and reshelving the books with the older titles. Not only do we do this for our segregated Fiction and genre collections, we also mark new Large Type books and new audio books with a dot on the spine. These dots are also removed after a set time period, but these books are always intershelved with the older titles, rather than in a separate area. (These collections are small enough to allow browsing without actually shelving new titles separately.) Whether the new titles are shelved separately or simply marked in smaller collections, readers really appreciate being able to identify the newer titles. The minimal shelver time the process takes is well worthwhile in terms of patron satisfaction.

Genre Collections

Segregated genre collections seem to be the new wave in many fiction collections. We've always held back from creating too many separate collections, believing they can be confusing to both staff and patrons. For example, can you always decide if a book is a romance or not unless you read it? (At least with Mystery, Science Fiction, and Fantasy one can often tell from the description, but, depending on how you define a romance, there could be problems.) And if you create too many collections, readers won't know where to look for their favorite authors. Will Bernard Cornwell's Sharpe series be with Historical Fiction or Military Fiction or perhaps Adventure? Titles by authors who write in several genres might be spread among a number of collections, making locating books more difficult for staff and readers.

On the other hand, segregation of collections can be very effective in creating smaller areas for patrons to browse and in grouping genre titles for ease of access. I only caution against going overboard. We have separate collections for Mystery and Science Fiction/Fantasy. When our building project is complete, we will also have a separate Western section for fans of that genre who came out of the woodwork when we integrated those titles into the fiction collection to save space. The Science Fiction/ Fantasy collection has had a life of its own. Originally, we had both genres together but traditionally called the collection Science Fiction. When Fantasy came into its own in the late 1980s and Fantasy readers at my library became more vocal, we decided to try to please them by separating out the Fantasy, putting a label on the spine, and interfiling it in with the Fiction. Finding Fantasy amidst rows and rows of novels was just a bad dream compared to the nightmare of trying to decide what was fantasy and what was science fiction. We finally decided to integrate the two collections again and call it Science Fiction/Fantasy. (This was one of those times when it paid to be on good terms with Technical Services!) Amazingly, most readers seem quite happy with the solution.

The main obstacle to segregating collections is creating guidelines to use in cataloging. These are vital, because you can't read every book you get and decide where to catalog it. Technical Services needs detailed guidelines, or they will expect you to make a separate decision about each title. (For example, for our paperback Romance collection Technical Services adds only those titles that have Romance as a noun on the book's spine. Thus, Historical Romance is included but not Romantic Suspense.) Or worse, they will catalog titles where they think they go. Even when you have guidelines, there will be questions. On the other hand, patrons love genre collections. Unfortunately, they expect to find the authors that they consider part of a genre, whether you think they are or not. We have created separate genre sections and will continue to do so, knowing, however, that we'll never please everyone.

One way to discover the characteristics of a genre that allow you to separate it from general fiction is to undertake a genre study. There is information on this in *Serving Readers*[3] and in the revised edition of *Readers' Advisory Service in the Public Library*.[4] Basically, the extensive reading in a genre and talking about our discoveries with staff and patrons make us more aware of a genre's pattern, its popularity, and its key authors. Sharing our discoveries with readers–both circulating titles and genre reference books–allows us to open the collection to a greater audience.

Displays

Readers like small collections of books; unless they're looking for a particular author or title, it's so much easier to browse that way. Because we can't sensibly create these mini-collections permanently, we offer displays of books, collected to highlight a subject or simply to expose less popular authors and titles. We have display cases designated for month-long displays of fiction on a particular topic: Cozy Mysteries or Books for a Long Winter's Night, for example. The value of displays in set places is that readers become accustomed to seeing books there on a variety of subjects. We also have a permanent display of Good Books You May Have Missed, filled by staff on the desk with less popular titles readers may not have discovered. Displays don't need to be elaborate, but they do need to have "quality" titles. We try to use the best we know in whatever genre or subject, so readers feel they can depend on the titles on the display.

Among our most popular displays are those that highlight books other readers have loved. That's one reason the Good Books You May Have Missed display has been so popular for so many years. Another very successful (and easy to set up) display along these lines features favorites read by participants in our Adult Summer Reading Club. Each year when they turn in lists of the books they read, they star the one they enjoyed the most. Our high school aides create a list of these favorites, and every May and June, as an advertisement for the club, we fill a display with these titles. They fly off the shelf! (This is the same phenomenon that draws readers to the shelves or trucks of just-returned books. Since someone else read them, they must be worth perusal and perhaps check-out.)

We also have a display unit that allows us to feature an assortment of book lists and bookmarks without the books. (Ours is free-standing, but I have seen others mounted on the end of a shelving range, and some libraries simply stack bookmarks and book lists on service desks or circulation counters to make them available.) This is an easy way to publicize your collection and to let patrons know you believe fiction is important.

Bookmarks and Annotated Book Lists

Bookmarks and annotated book lists also highlight collections, but creating them takes more staff time. Again, they provide interested readers with a smaller universe of books to choose from, as well as a list to take home with them. One of my favorites is our Recent Fiction bookmark. One of the staff produces it biannually, and it highlights, with one-sentence annotations, interesting newer books that weren't best sellers. Book lists and bookmarks help staff, too, when we're working with a reader who enjoys books on a topic we have covered in a list, or when our minds go blank.

Books in Series and Award-Winners

Over the past few years, we've begun indicating that a book is an award-winner (Pulitzer, Hugo, ALA Books for Reluctant Readers, etc.) by stamping the pocket "Award Winner" and indicating the award. I'm always grateful for this information when I'm weeding. Having it right on the book means I don't have to check every title elsewhere to make certain I'm not weeding something we need to keep. Patrons also appreciate seeing that the book they're considering has won a special award. It's somehow an assurance of quality, even though it doesn't mean that they will personally enjoy the book.

We also stamp the pockets of series books, and give the number of the book in the series and the title of the series. As series are becoming more and more popular, readers appreciate seeing that they have chosen volume one, so they can start at the beginning, or that they have chosen a later volume and need to find the first. Both of these procedures require little initial effort and save us time on a daily basis as we work with patrons.

Talking About Books

Finally, talking about books informally among staff and also more formally with patrons is as important in opening the collection to users as it is in helping us discover what to purchase. When we share books with fellow staff, we learn what they're reading and what we can pass along to patrons, without actually reading the book. When we talk with readers, we introduce them to new authors or parts of the collection they likely would never discover on their own. It's one of the most important things we do.

Fiction acquisition is more than physically selecting and acquiring titles for a library collection. The best acquisition is done by staff who work the desk and interact, on a daily basis, with library users and staff. Selectors can no longer afford to isolate themselves and purchase only what they think best for their fiction collections.

When patrons and all staff become active participants in the entire acquisition process, they, and the library, benefit. Not only is the collection better, more closely representing the materials that are needed, but we public service staff are better able to *serve* our patrons. We're comfortable in our ability to provide the titles they seek, because we have developed strategies to solicit that information. The library's reading public are more comfortable seeking our assistance, because they know we value their opinions. In today's public libraries, we need to form a partnership between patrons and staff (*all* staff, whether public service or not, selectors or not) to provide materials readers want now, as well as those that form the foundation of an excellent fiction collection that withstands the vicissitudes of popularity and time.

NOTES

1. *The Downers Grove Public Library Bylaws, Policies, and Guidelines*, n.d., unpaged.
2. ibid.
3. *Serving Readers*, ed. Ted Balcom. Fort Atkinson, WI: Highsmith Press, 1997.
4. Saricks, Joyce and Brown, Nancy. *Readers' Advisory Service in the Public Library*. 2nd ed. Chicago: American Library Association, 1997.

Using Local Marketing Characteristics to Customize the Conspectus for Fiction Assessment

Burns Davis

SUMMARY. There are several possible ways to assess fiction, biography, and biographical fiction collections using accepted conspectus methods. This article recommends that the choice of method be guided by the meaningful collection groupings that are used by a local library to provide access to its resources. Since these arrangements are usually related to the ways customers use the library and to the strategies employed by the library to market its collection, they suggest ways to organize assessment data and relate the data to acquisitions activities. WLN conspectus software flexibility enables librarians to produce customized assessment results by using technique and tool adaptions based on local collection arrangement. *[Article copies available for a fee from The Haworth Document Delivery Service: 1-800-342-9678. E-mail address: getinfo@haworth.com]*

INTRODUCTION

Management of collection assessments to adapt conspectus usage to provide relevant information about local service patterns is the focus of this article. Possible options for organizing assessment data for fiction

Burns Smith Davis is Information Resources Coordinator, Nebraska Library Commission, 1200 N Street, Suite 120, Lincoln, NE 68508-2023.

[Haworth co-indexing entry note]: "Using Local Marketing Characteristics to Customize the Conspectus for Fiction Assessment." Davis, Burns. Co-published simultaneously in *The Acquisitions Librarian* (The Haworth Press, Inc.) No. 19, 1998, pp. 29-44; and: *Fiction Acquisition/Fiction Management: Education and Training* (ed: Georgine N. Olson) The Haworth Press, Inc., 1998, pp. 29-44. Single or multiple copies of this article are available for a fee from The Haworth Document Delivery Service [1-800-342-9678, 9:00 a.m. - 5:00 p.m. (EST)]. E-mail address: getinfo@haworth.com].

29

resources are suggested and a recently completed assessment at a small public library is used as an example. The example illustrates the implementation of a locally created fiction division and recommends some ideas for adapting fiction categories to local purposes across special collection and marketing groups, reading levels, and formats.

Two main aspects of the assessment process with the following points are discussed:

Technique and tool adaptions
1. Locally created conspectus divisions
   - Adult and Juvenile fiction
   - Special areas of the collection such as reference, biography, and local history materials
2. Interdisciplinary divisions
3. Reports grouping conspectus lines into special interest areas by using macros for data entry in searchable comments fields

Customized results
1. Reports related to specific customer groups or service objectives
2. Reports describing collection management action needed
3. Reports related to budget planning

MARKETING (CUSTOMER SERVICE) IS RELATED TO ASSESSMENT ORGANIZATION

Annual nationwide comparative statistics for public libraries in the Public Library Association's annual *Public Library Data Service Statistical Report*[1] and R.R. Bowker's *Bowker Annual Library and Book Trade Almanac*[2] report substantial fiction title counts that comprise as much as half of public library resources. School and academic libraries also collect fiction materials in quantity. In public libraries especially, fiction collections are often not classified according to Dewey or Library of Congress numbers. Instead, fiction materials are commonly shelved in genre, format, or reading level sections which are organized alphabetically by authors' names. Due to the lack of classification and due to the locally varied arrangements of these materials on libraries' shelves, fiction collection arrangements are less easily correlated than nonfiction to formal analytical structures such as the WLN Conspectus.[3] However, fiction collections are important resources especially in small- and medium-sized public libraries where fiction materials may be the busiest and most numerous materials in the library.

In a public library it is possible for the fiction collection to represent half or more of the total resources, and fiction materials may comprise 50% or more of the library's circulation. To limit an assessment to nonfiction would present an incomplete picture of the library's resources. Therefore, it is particularly important that helpful alternatives are available for libraries to assess their fiction materials. This article presents a method for tailoring fiction assessment to local marketing needs, collection groupings, and special formats. This type of assessment which is based on how the library collection is marketed might be called a service-oriented assessment.

Marketing should be a substantial part of the basis for assessing a collection of library resources.[4] Marketing in the sense it is used in this article refers to the ways librarians serve their customers: the way information and recreation materials are arranged to catch the attention of library customers and make it easy for customers to find what they want, how the library's role as defined by its mission is filled, and how the library is promoted.

People "shop" for books in the library in ways similar to the ways they shop for books in stores.[5] The arrangement of a library's collection will, by conscious plan or not, usually reflect something about who the target audience is and what they are seeking. Fiction materials in the library come closest in use, selection, and display to the marketing environment of a commercial bookstore which attempts to place materials where they can be easily located by customers because the materials are grouped according to the customers' special interests.[6] Fiction materials are often shelved by genres and formats: the way the items are used in customer service. A natural process would be for assessment and management of these materials to follow these groupings.

Fiction can be classified within the Dewey Decimal or Library of Congress classification schedules, but libraries often do not use these classification schedules to organize resources; choosing instead to arrange materials in units related to the way their customers look for them. These sections tend to be much like the genre and format arrangements found in commercial bookstores. Biography can be assessed with the 920s or CTs in the HID027-027.8 or HIS020-023 line numbers of the conspectus, and American fiction with the 813s or PS and PZ1-4s in the LAD230-235 or LLL250-263 line numbers. Fiction in other languages and in English translation would be assessed in other line numbers. This organization seems most useful to large public or academic libraries, and is less related to the way smaller public and school libraries organize and use their fiction materials. Several models of fiction assessment by genre and format have been suggested which seem easy to use and to explain.[7] No single "best way" has yet come to be the standard way to assess a library's fiction collection. Since the assessment data needs to be collected in a way that will produce subject-related reports that are useful to the library, it may be necessary for the assessment project coordinator to build local subject divisions or select searchable comments notes that can produce customized conspectus reports for the local assessment.[8]

Assessing a library collection is a process of taking as accurate a picture as possible of what resources the library has to support its service to customers. It is important to be able to evaluate and retrieve information about the collection that is presented in a fashion which corresponds to the way the collection is marketed: the ways customers use and find library resources. Selection and weeding are also likely to be performed in relation to customer usage. Comparing the picture of what the resources are now to what resources are needed to meet the goal suggests what action should be taken. To successfully complete a collection evaluation, an assessment project will adapt quantitative and qualitative measurements in a way that will provide facts about local characteristics. Clearly stating what the assessment needs to tell about the local collection is the place to start in adapting the standardized measurements. Assessing the collection focuses the librarian's vision on what is really there so that the most effective selections can be made for acquisitions of materials that directly support customer service, thereby meeting marketing objectives.

In a time of concern with customer service, collection assessment should include the library's environment because assessing the relevance of the library's holdings to its service monitors the extent to which a library's collection is in harmony with its mission.[9] Regardless of whether the arrangement is planned or is a response to use in practice, the way a collection is organized will usually reflect patterns that say something about how customers look for materials. The most important thing is that the collection be described and evaluated in ways relevant to how library customers use the library, which is, hopefully, the same as how the library serves its customers.

TECHNIQUE AND TOOL ADAPTIONS

Methods

The flexibility of the conspectus method provides the opportunity to utilize local quantitative data and to tailor the process to the staff available for the project. Special aspects of the collection that relate to local service patterns and outstanding areas of the library materials collection may be profiled either by assessing selected categories or subjects within existing divisions, by adding local divisions to the conspectus, or by adding uniform notes in the WLN Conspectus comments field that may be used to compile reports or interdisciplinary divisions. These are the primary choices for assessing fiction collections using the conspectus method with the WLN Conspectus software:

- use the language, literature, and linguistics, or history division lines that correlate to the Dewey Decimal or Library of Congress classification schedules for fiction literature;
- enter keywords in the comments field that will generate an interdisciplinary division or report; or
- create a local division for fiction that includes genre and format categories appropriate to the library.

Fiction is treated in the Dewey version of the conspectus by periods such as *Colonial Period* or *Post Revolutionary Period in American and English Literature*. In the Library of Congress version of the conspectus fiction is assigned as a *Fiction in English* category, as *Juvenile Literature* by language, or in the category *American Literature Since 1961* with genres as subjects. Historical fiction may be recorded in the appropriate history subjects or separated as a category in a fiction division, depending on the library's customer usage. Fiction may also be dealt with as a *Fiction* category at the end of divisions or categories as in the following examples:

HISTORY

    Fiction

or

BIOLOGY

    Fiction

or

HISTORY

    Biography, Genealogy, Insignia

    Fiction

However, the previous method would not easily allow report generation of fiction lines together in the body of conspectus proof reports. The assessment data in the existing conspectus structure would be primarily recorded in lines correlated to a classification scheme (Dewey or LC) that is not generally employed by the library for those materials. Separate comments searches or interdisciplinary files would need to be created in order to report fiction as a group.

Conspectus categories correlated to LC or Dewey classification schedules may not be similar to the way fiction is arranged in many small library collections that are unclassified. Using a locally created division for fiction particularly highlights the marketing segment priorities within a local library. It is appropriate for use in assessing a small library's collection of adult and juvenile fiction, and may also be used in larger libraries. The methods used for collecting and organizing data, and for generating printed reports follow accepted assessment practice. The WLN Conspectus software was employed in the example library.

Locally Created Conspectus Divisions

A locally created division lifts fiction up to view so it can be examined on the same level with major nonfiction portions of the collection. Although a locally created division may possibly sacrifice uniformity in cooperative collection development data sharing, its advantage is in its ability to neatly assemble data about fiction collection genres and formats. It also presents the fiction data at the level of other divisions; keeping the relative importance of all fiction materials equal with nonfiction in supporting library service delivery to customers. Data about fiction materials can then be manipulated utilizing the full range of features of the WLN Conspectus software for showing the data on printed results in text and graph reports. The reporting options are somewhat more limited if data is handled in interdisciplinary divisions or in the searchable comments field.

Flexibility is the key to arriving at workable assessment solutions. The wealth of possible ways to assess collections and the possible details of information that can be collected could be overwhelming and could cause the significance of an assessment to be lost. It is necessary to carefully choose what is important to know and eliminate all else. Most librarians will have very little time to prepare for an assessment. The time spent needs to produce relevant results quickly. Connecting materials in the collection with customers is usually the most important outcome desired for fiction materials. Most libraries buy fiction titles intending them to be located quickly and used often. The way many libraries market fiction materials is directed toward customers' interests: finding the materials and checking them out, appealing to impulse shoppers. If assessment is to help librarians see what the supply of materials is and what their usage is, it makes sense to organize data collection and reports in groups that correlate to the library's own marketing characteristics.

This can be accomplished by using the supple features of the conspectus method and WLN Conspectus software. Taking advantage of the opportunities offered by the following possibilities built into the method and software:

> local divisions
> macros
> searchable comments
> spreadsheet data collection
> design of assessment purpose
> management information file

Adapting Existing Conspectus Structure to Local Collection Groupings

Report features are built into the WLN Conspectus software. Uniform notes recorded in the comments field are searchable and reports can be printed from these notes. To use notes, analyze factors during shelf observation that are key to the collection management objectives and record these characteristics using selected keywords as uniform notes. Examples of terms that will generate useful reports from searchable comments are median age, ILL, update, weed, summer reading program, or genre labels.

Another possibility is to add genres as subject lines in the literature categories. Existing conspectus categories which may be used for fiction and biography assessment are listed below.

Dewey			Library of Congress	
Conspectus line	Class #	Heading	Conspectus line	Class #
HID027-HID027.8	(920)	Biography	HIS020-023	(CT1-3830)
LAD230-235	(813)	Fiction		
		Amer. Lit.-1961-	LLL250-263	(PS3550-3576)
		[Includes genres as subjects LLL258-262]		
		Fiction in English	LLL490	(PZ1-4)

Special Collection Groupings and Formats

Any unique categories that are appropriate for local customer service may be accommodated in the conspectus without eroding the validity of the assessment process or results. Assessment is intended to be based on a clearly-stated collection management policy. The selection of what data to collect is oriented to which portions of the collection have greatest priority to the library's mission, are most numerous, are most used by library customers, and are most relevant to the way assessment results will be used.

The factors that can be used to plan special collections or fiction materials assessment are:

> shelflist order and cataloging
> shelf display
> reading level separations
> circulation counting procedures
> collection management policy selection criteria
> purchasing and weeding data record keeping procedures
> local library fiction subdivision terminology
> collection subunits
> service objectives for fiction materials
> record keeping about program use

The Fiction Division

To assess fiction as a distinct division of the collection, information is entered about the library's fiction collection in worksheets using a locally created division in the WLN Conspectus. Instructions for adding divisions to the conspectus are provided in the software manual. The conspectus reports will then separate the fiction divisions from nonfiction divisions. In this approach, adult and juvenile reading levels may be treated separately or together. In the example library, the reading levels were treated as separate fiction divisions.

Many librarians devise sections in their fiction collection for the convenience of their patrons. Some of the most commonly used groups are listed as follows. These may be used as category and subject headings in a locally created fiction division. Category headings that follow section titles in the library's collection might also be feasible. Assessment worksheets and division comparison reports may be printed for locally created divisions.

Reading Levels	Adult
	Young Adult
	Juvenile
	Easy Readers and Picture books
	High/Low

Genres	Adventure	Biographical fiction
	General fiction	Horror fiction
	Mystery	Western fiction
	Romance	Historical fiction
	Science fiction	Short Stories
	Fantasy	Other
	Classic fiction	

Formats	Hardcover book
	Paperbound book
	Large print book
	Videotape
	Audio book
	Electronic databases, CD-ROM, software
	Braille

The holdings information, median age, condition of the materials, program support, collection development action to be taken, and any other important information may be incorporated in the comments column of the conspectus worksheets. Alternately, the librarian may choose to treat significant collections related to reading levels as interdisciplinary divisions of the conspectus. Instructions for coding assessment data for interdisciplinary divisions and for producing searchable comments reports are provided in the WLN Conspectus software manual. Using a uniform vocabulary for information that is noted in the comments field permits the use of macros for entering data and facilitates sorting comments reports. Collection depth indicators are standardized, numerical codes which permit comparison of the actual collection to goals. Assigning these indicators also permits comparisons between libraries. Instructions for assigning the collection depth indicators for fiction are included in the *WLN Conspectus Handbook*.[10]

The points to consider in reviewing the collection, noting significant features, and assigning collection depth indicators are the same for fiction and special collection sections as those for other areas of the collection:

- The universe of publication and the scope of the division
- The library's collection in relation to holdings in other libraries
- Access to the collection
- Physical characteristics of the resources
- Use of the collection
- The nature of the subject literature and types of materials appropriate to the subject

A PUBLIC LIBRARY EXAMPLE

Here is an example of how an assessment project adapted the conspectus to fit a public library which serves a community of 9,700. The desired outcome was to show what curriculum support materials are available and what will be needed, what resources in volumes and dollars will be needed to develop the collection, how well the space allowed in a new building will be used and its adequacy, and what weeding can be done in the collection.

The entire library collection was assessed including uncataloged and cataloged resources in all formats and all reading levels. Information about the collection was gathered from use data, shelf observation, and shelflist measurement. In general, the collection was assessed at the division level. Children's nonfiction materials are intershelved with adult materials and were assessed in the standard conspectus lines. Outstanding areas of the collection that relate to local service patterns were profiled either by assessing selected categories or subjects within divisions, by adding local divisions to the conspectus, or by adding uniform notes in the WLN Conspectus comments field. Uniform notes in the comments field are searchable and reports were printed from these notes. Initially interdisciplinary divisions were planned for "Nebraskana" (local history) and curriculum support materials. Instead, searchable comments were used because the reports produced from them were satisfactory and were simpler to manipulate than interdisciplinary divisions. Adding a quick note to the conspectus line as assessors located relevant materials during shelf observation proved to be the most effective way to identify materials related to local history and curriculum support. These materials are partially shelved as a unit, but most are scattered throughout the collection.

The flexibility of the conspectus software and resilience of the assessment techniques enabled us to adapt the conspectus structure as necessary for the local environment and still produce a valid and thorough assessment for this small library. Its data can then be compared with other libraries' results in the database.

Listed here are the local divisions and the customized reports generated from comments in the notes fields. The locally created divisions match service categories of important, high-use sections of the collection. In this library these divisions include many unclassified and uncataloged materials and nonprint formats. The customized reports are generated from comments in the notes fields. They are produced by searching on a uniform note keyword and then printing the listed conspectus lines with their assessment information. Three types of reports were used: reports about resources in special formats or about specific services, reports about collection development action to be taken, and reports about customer use. The list of reports prepared from uniform notes is shown as an example of what is possible. The uniform notes utilize terms chosen by the library staff as meaningful in their daily work.

LOCAL DIVISIONS/CATEGORIES/SUBJECTS

The arrangement in this list indicates the hierarchical order of headings in the conspectus: DIVISION
Category
Subject
ADULT FICTION
Adult Fiction
   Adventure
   General
   Mystery
   Romance
   Science Fiction and Fantasy
   Horror
   Western
   Historical
Adult Paperback Rack
   General Fiction
   Novels
   Miscellaneous
   Romance
   Western
Audio Books
JUVENILE FICTION
Juvenile Fiction General
Juvenile Paperback

Juvenile Easy
Easy Cassettes
REFERENCE
HOLIDAY

CUSTOMIZED REPORTS

FORMATS AND SERVICES
Audio Books
CD-ROM
Electronic Information Resources
Videos
Vertical File
Nebraskana (Local History)
Curriculum Support
Reference
Summer Reading Program
COLLECTION DEVELOPMENT ACTION
Weed
Update or Replace
Add
USE REPORTS
Interlibrary Loan Borrowed
Circulation

Use Data

Collating comments and calculating quantitative data was accomplished on spreadsheets before recording data on the conspectus worksheets and entering them into the database. Interlibrary loan statistics reported by Dewey call number were correlated to WLN Conspectus divisions and entered in the comments field of the WLN Conspectus.

Circulation statistics had been recorded by Dewey 100 numbers on the library's monthly reports. For the assessment the Dewey 100 numbers were correlated as closely as possible to relevant WLN Conspectus divisions and entered in the comments field of the WLN Conspectus. Per item circulation in this library is much higher than average so median ages collected during the shelf observation were verified with median ages taken from shelflist sampling. Reference statistics were not included in this assessment because data about reference questions are not recorded in a form which permits useful subject correlation to the conspectus. Sampling may be considered during the next assessment.

Results

The library profile data from the *Nebraska Public Library Profile 1993-1994 Statistical Data*, Nebraska Library Commission, April, 1996, show that the number of items owned in this collection are proportionately small in relation to the high circulation. The overall materials expenditure is quite low for a library of this size and circulation volume. However, there is annual weeding during which a moderate number of materials are withdrawn, and titles are regularly added to several key areas of the collection.

The assessment results confirmed that maintenance is taking place and also pointed out areas where older materials are sitting on shelves. In comparing the plans for the new library with assessment reports, several characteristics stood out. The staff work areas, collection shelving, and storage spaces seemed considerably underestimated in the building plans. The library would actually experience space challenges from its opening day. Assessment reports identified key areas that need updating and weeding, allowing the librarian to plan budget requests and collection maintenance activities before the move. The librarian will also use the assessment results to plan the most effective shelving arrangement in the new space. The assessment reports were used by the library staff and library board as supporting documentation to explain budget requests and building needs to the City Council and the community.

Project Evaluation

To gain an idea of how well the assessment project met their needs, the staff were asked to share their ideas about what worked and what they would change. In a final group meeting the staff expressed the following impressions of their experience during the project:

- On the first day there was much apprehension and feeling of inadequacy. However, in carrying on with the assessment work assignments they developed an appreciation for what they knew and a feeling that the project could be done.
- It was very helpful to assess the entire collection.
- Using the analogy of comparing the assessment process to "taking a picture" of the collection was helpful.
- All staff learned a lot about the collection that will help them do their jobs better.

Assessment Benefits–Testimonial from the Field

In many libraries, fiction materials may be the busiest in the collection. The purposes of performing an assessment at the example library were to describe the status of the collection and to collect data that would support a budget plan for developing the library's resources. During the assessment process shelflist date sampling and shelf observation techniques were also adapted to verify median age to use in a high circulation per item environment. The library in the case study began using the results of their assessment immediately to set weeding priorities and to estimate space needs for moving the collection to a new facility. Even as the shelf observations were taking place during the assessment project, staff were identifying sections that needed selecting and weeding attention. These observations were collected and reported in the searchable comments field of the WLN Conspectus. The uses of space in the proposed new building and the construction plans were reviewed to determine if there is adequate shelf room, if there are potential physical hazards to library materials, and if the space layouts are well-arranged for public access and service. The librarian, who regularly attends to her collection's maintenance by selecting new materials and weeding, knows her community thoroughly, and has many years of service experience in this library, summed the assessment benefits very well:

> I learned so much about the collection. It [the assessment] really gave me a better idea about what to DO!

CONCLUSION

Choosing an assessment approach that adapts the conspectus structure to local library practice is useful for organizing assessment information about resources in the collection that are arranged by:

- specialized local interest,
- format,
- genre, or
- usage (customer group).

Resources typically arranged in these kinds of units are often not classified by Dewey or Library of Congress schedules, and may be uncataloged. These local groupings are practical relationships that usually reflect something about the service delivery given by the library. Types of materials often handled in functional subdivisions are:

- fiction
- biography
- biographical fiction
- nonprint formats
- local interest collections
- children's materials, and
- adaptive formats such as large type.

The innate flexibility of the conspectus method enables assessors to emulate local organization of these types of resources in assessment reports. A choice may be made from locally created divisions, interdisciplinary divisions, and reports generated from searchable comments. Results obtained from assessing library collections in a method that reflects local library service patterns may more strongly support decision making based on client service. In this way the adaptive power of the conspectus tools may be more fully employed, and assessing librarians are encouraged to use it to their advantage.

REFERENCES

1. *Public Library Data Service Statistical Report*. Chicago: Public Library Association, 1988- . [Annual].

2. *The Bowker Annual Library and Book Trade Almanac*. 41st ed. New Providence, NJ: R.R. Bowker, 1911/12- . [Annual].

3. WLN. *WLN Conspectus Software Version 6.2 for Windows*. Lacey, WA: WLN, 1997.

4. Baker, Sharon L. "Quality and Demand: The Basis for Fiction Collection Assessment." *Collection Building*, 13:2-3, 1994, 65-8.

5. Scheppke, Jim. "Who's Using the Public Library?" *Library Journal*, 119:17, October 15, 1994, 35-37.

6. Baker, Sharon L. *The Responsive Public Library Collection: How to Develop and Market It*. Englewood, CO: Libraries Unlimited, Inc., 1993.

7. Bushing, Mary; Davis, Burns; and Powell, Nancy. *WLN Conspectus Handbook*. Lacey, WA: WLN, 1997. [In Press].

Baker, Sharon L., and Boze, Patricia J. *Fiction Collection Assessment Manual*. Champaign, IL: Lincoln Trail Libraries System, 1992.

Graham, Ruth. *Collection Profile, Acquisitions, Budget Manual*. Aukland, NZ: North Shore City Council, 1992.

8. Davis, Burns. "Designing a Fiction Assessment Tool: The Customer Service Approach." In Georgine N. Olson and Barbara McFadden Allen, Eds. *Coop-

erative Collection Management: The Conspectus Approach. New York: Neal-Schuman Publishers, Inc., 1994.

9. Senkevitch, Judith J., and Sweetland, James H. "Evaluating Adult Fiction in the Smaller Public Library." *RQ*, 34:1, Fall 1994, 78-89.

10. Bushing, Mary; Davis, Burns; and Powell, Nancy. *WLN Conspectus Handbook.* Lacey, WA: WLN, 1997. [In Press].

Options for Fiction Provision
in Academic Libraries:
Book Lease Plans

Janelle M. Zauha

SUMMARY. Book lease plans are a viable option for the provision of fiction and other recreational reading materials in the academic library. Traditionally used by public libraries as a means of providing multiple copies of bestsellers and reducing long hold lists, lease plans are used by some academic libraries because they are convenient, flexible alternatives to the selection and development of elaborate popular reading collections. Two popular book lease programs are described and compared. A 1997 follow-up survey of libraries using lease plans in 1976 shows that, despite their flexible and affordable nature, these collections may fall on hard times unless they are carefully promoted, justified, and creatively funded. *[Article copies available for a fee from The Haworth Document Delivery Service: 1-800-342-9678. E-mail address: getinfo@haworth.com]*

"And what are you reading, Miss ___?" "Oh! it is only a novel!" replies the young lady; while she lays down her book with affected indifference, or momentary shame.–"It is only Cecilia, or Camilla, or Belinda"; or, in short, only some work in which the greatest powers of the mind are displayed, in which the most thorough

Janelle M. Zauha is Assistant Professor, Reference Librarian and Electronic Information Coordinator, The Libraries, Montana State University-Bozeman, P.O. Box 173320, Bozeman, MT 59717-3320.

[Haworth co-indexing entry note]: "Options for Fiction Provision in Academic Libraries: Book Lease Plans." Zauha, Janelle M. Co-published simultaneously in *The Acquisitions Librarian* (The Haworth Press, Inc.) No. 19, 1998, pp. 45-54; and: *Fiction Acquisition/Fiction Management: Education and Training* (ed: Georgine N. Olson) The Haworth Press, Inc., 1998, pp. 45-54. Single or multiple copies of this article are available for a fee from The Haworth Document Delivery Service [1-800-342-9678, 9:00 a.m. - 5:00 p.m. (EST)]. E-mail address: getinfo@haworth.com.

knowledge of human nature, the happiest delineation of its varieties,
the liveliest effusions of wit and humour are conveyed to the world
in the best chosen language.

—Jane Austen, *Northanger Abbey*

Demands on the academic library to meet curricular needs and to supply the expensive equipment necessary to access electronic information
are financially absorbing, to say the least. As higher education moves
relentlessly toward implementation of the business principle of the bottom
line, costs must constantly be examined and measured against tangible
returns. It is little wonder, then, that the academic library is able to devote
few funds, if any, toward the collection of fiction for the extracurricular
reading needs of students, faculty, and staff. Those libraries who do have
funds earmarked for "recreational reading" or "browsing room" collections find this budget line increasingly difficult to justify. The very phrases
used to describe such collections suggest superfluity and inefficiency and
certainly do not trumpet their value to the curriculum.

In a society leery of the benefits of fiction reading by adolescents or
adults, especially fiction of the "popular" variety, the high proportion of
popular fiction in such collections makes them all the more suspect. This
suspicion is deeply embedded, having almost as long a tradition as fiction
itself. Libraries themselves have helped perpetuate it. As Paul Sturges and
Alison Barr point out, not only has the value of fiction reading been
downplayed, it has been viewed as a nuisance.[1] This attitude is subtly
manifested today in libraries of all types where catalog access to fiction
through subject headings is difficult at best. Further evidence of our disin-
clination to seriously consider fiction's place in the library (despite its high
circulation) is the lack of published research that deals with its selection,
evaluation, and use, even in the area where it is most prominent and
popular, the public library.[2]

The combined effects of tight money, insistence on tangible returns,
and a cultural prejudice against popular fiction have meant lean times for
recreational or browsing collections in academic libraries. For those academic libraries that have managed to develop and support such collections, the popularity and prominence of the collections may actually make
them more vulnerable. Recreational reading collections are high profile
because of their locations in the library (often visible on the first floor or
from main service areas) and because of their patent difference from the
rest of the curriculum-focused academic collection. They are often viewed
as superfluous and the result has been a steady whittling away of the
popular reading collections, facilities, and services of such prominent

academic institutions as the University of Illinois at Urbana-Champaign and the University of Iowa.[3]

Is there no hope, then, for the academic library that cannot afford politically, spatially, or financially to devote significant resources to the extra-curricular reading interests of students, faculty and staff? Some libraries have discovered a viable option for provision of recreational reading in the use of book lease plans. Lease plans have traditionally been used by public libraries to provide multiple copies of bestsellers and reduce long hold lists. Academic libraries as well have found book lease plans to be convenient, flexible alternatives to the selection and development of elaborate popular reading collections. While these collections represent a fairly low-level of commitment in terms of money and staff time, they, too, may fall on hard times unless they are carefully promoted, justified, and creatively funded.

ANATOMY OF A LEASE PLAN

Book lease plans allow libraries to rent new books, in effect, with the option to purchase titles at a reduced cost after leasing. Lease plans are attractive because they enable a library to use books that are popular for a time, fill the demand for them, and then cycle them out of the collection when their popularity has passed. This saves time, space, and money, while providing patrons with access to the latest high-profile books, whether fiction or nonfiction. Books received on lease plan require minimal processing and are usually kept separate from the main collection in prominent display areas. Both fiction and non-fiction are offered through lease plans, but fiction usually makes up the majority of the offerings.

The two most prominent book lease plans in operation today are the McNaughton Plan (Brodart) and Baker & Taylor's Book Leasing System.[4] The McNaughton Plan has been in place since the 1940s; Baker & Taylor's plan began in the mid-1980s. Although public libraries make up the bulk of the customers for these plans, both vendors work with academic libraries as well to supply adult recreational reading materials. The following overview of their services shows that the plans have many similarities; bulleted sections denote specific differences between the two vendor plans.

Contracts. The library enters into a yearly contract with the vendor. The contract is tailored to the needs and size of the library. Different contract types may be offered, based on point or book quotas, and new or used books. The contract establishes the size of the core collection and the number of books a library may select to add to that collection each month.

- *McNaughton:* Book plan options start at 5 books per month, $867 per year; economy point options start at 10 books per month, $420 per year; minimum contract commitment is 1 year and 60 days cancellation notice after that.
- *Baker & Taylor:* Book plan options start at 10 books per month, $1,788 per year; point plan options start at 30 points per month, $594 per year; no minimum contract commitment is required and cancellation notice is negotiable.

Core Collection. When a library begins a lease plan, it usually selects an initial set of books from the vendor's core list to serve as a basic collection.

- *McNaughton:* The size of the basic collection is usually 20 times the monthly service level agreed upon in the contract.
- *Baker & Taylor:* The size of the basic collection is usually 10 times the monthly service level.

Monthly Selections. The library selects a quota of books each month to add to its basic collection. Selections are made from the vendor's monthly prepublication list and from a list of in-stock bestsellers and other popular books. The prepublication list includes information on books to be published in the next 2-3 months, such as annotations, author information, promotional information, print runs, and media tie-ins like author appearances on the *Today* show. Titles are chosen for the prepublication list by buyers and/or a board of librarians, booksellers and vendor editors from review sources such as the *New York Times Bestsellers List, Library Journal, Kirkus Reviews, Booklist,* and *Publishers Weekly.* Libraries may select books not on the monthly list.

- *McNaughton:* Books appear on prepublication list 3 months prior to publication; a selection service is offered for the basic collection and for monthly selections based on a library profile; a library selects 20% of its core per month; selection categories in the monthly prepublication list include nonfiction, general fiction, genre fiction (with titles denoted M, R, SF, or FF), special selection, large print, and reference books.
- *Baker & Taylor:* Books appear on prepublication list 2 months prior to publication; a selection service is not offered; a library selects 10% of its core per month; selection categories in the monthly prepublication list include biography, general nonfiction, adventure and suspense, general fiction, historical fiction, horror, mystery, romance, science fiction, and fantasy.

Returns, Purchase/Retention, Lost/Damaged Books. The library returns or purchases items from its core collection at various points during the contract year.

- *McNaughton:* Books are returned at the discretion of the library, not at specific times; books may be purchased from the collection (rather than returned) at any time for 75% off retail price; during semi-annual volume discount sales, a library may purchase titles out of its own current inventory for as little as $2 per book; an additional discount of 2% on annual prepayments is offered; in the case of loss or damage, a library may claim up to 2% of its annual new book allowance at no charge.
- *Baker & Taylor:* Books are returned monthly or quarterly, when basic collection is exceeded by 25%; 1 book may be kept for every 5 returned, others may be purchased at 75% discount; an additional discount of 2% on annual prepayment is offered, and 1% on semi-annual prepayment; in the case of loss or damage, there is no additional charge to the library.

Shipping, Processing. Shipping charges for the core collection, for monthly selections and for returns are paid by the vendor. The method of shipment is usually RPS or UPS within 48 hours of receipt of order when the title is from the vendor's in-stock list. Books arrive "shelf ready," including clear plastic covers and a range of other options, including catalog records in card or electronic format, book pockets, spine and bar code labels.

ACADEMIC LIBRARIES AND LEASE PLANS: MONTANA STATE UNIVERSITY

Little research has been done into the use of lease plans by academic libraries. A 1976 article by Ruth Carol Cushman reported survey responses from 14 academic libraries using lease plans.[5] At that time, Cushman observed that "[p]ublic libraries have been taking advantage of these services for several years, but academic librarians are sometimes slow in descending from the ivory tower of academe and have been using lease services for only a few years–rather hesitantly and in small numbers, at that."[6] Paul B. Weiner's 1980 survey of the recreational reading services of 110 academic libraries revealed that 15 of 83 respondents, or 29.4%, leased books from a vendor at that time. Out of the entire survey, 61.4% said they provided recreational reading of some kind.[7]

Examination of the history of a lease plan at an academic library in Montana, one of the most budget-challenged states in the Union, affords a 1980s snapshot of the fluctuating fortunes of such plans.[8] The Libraries at Montana State University-Bozeman began use of a McNaughton plan in 1982 to supply materials for a new recreational reading collection. These books were displayed prominently in the first floor lobby area of Renne Library, the main university library. The McNaughton books were placed face-out on an eye-level shelf running along one side of the lobby and on one side of the adjoining catalog area. This shelving took optimal advantage of their attractive covers and ensured that they would be seen by anyone entering or leaving the library. In addition, the library's "Welcome" pamphlet briefly mentioned the collection and gave its location.

Catalog cards for the books were filed in the main library catalog. Monthly selections, withdrawals, and purchase decisions were made by the Book Selection Review Committee, a collections body made up of four members representing the circulation, technical services (acquisitions), reference, and special collections departments of the library. Selection suggestions from other library staff were also taken into consideration. At the end of each academic quarter, the collection was reviewed. Items on the shelves that had not circulated at least 5 times in the previous 3 months were removed and considered for purchase or return to McNaughton. Once a year, between the summer and autumn quarters, the collection was reviewed using the acquisition department's McNaughton shelflist to identify missing items. It was considered a fairly low-maintenance collection, since all the books arrived shelf ready and accompanied by catalog cards.

The collection proved very popular. While circulation data from those pre-automation days is not available, internal memoranda indicate that as of February of 1983, 85-90% were in circulation, leaving only 35-50 titles in the display area at any given time. This observation prompted an increase in the plan from 330 books at $4,086 per year to 440 books at $5,448 per year for the 1983/84 academic year. The dean of the libraries considered the collection a good public relations tool and an inexpensive way of adding select books to the main collection. The perception of those involved with the plan is that the heaviest use of the books came from university staff and faculty, but no data can be found to verify this observation.

By the 1985/86 academic year, over $6,200 was budgeted for the recreational reading collection, serving a student, faculty, and professional body numbering approximately 12,000, as reported in the 1984-86 university bulletin. Unfortunately, this was the beginning of some very lean budget years for the university and the library was asked in spring of 1986 to prepare to trim 10% from its budget for 1986/87. Despite the library's satisfaction with its McNaughton plan and the popularity of the collection, elimination of it was recommended by staff in both technical and public services in the first round of cuts.

Faced with the possibility of deep cuts to essential services, the library administration deemed that the recreational reading needs of the university could be better served by Bozeman Public Library. The plan was canceled as of July 1, 1986. Several staff suggested that a recreational reading collection be pieced together out of gift books and supplemented with the more "readable" books from the main collection. Continued budget cuts, however, precluded either the reinstatement of the McNaughton plan or the devotion of staff time to the development of an alternate recreational collection. New books purchased for the main collection were placed on the display shelf in the lobby and catalog area, with original covers intact, and continue to be shelved there today. Users requesting recreational reading materials are directed to Bozeman Public Library or the university bookstore.

SURVEYED LIBRARIES: 1976-1996

Beyond one library's tale of woe, there is some evidence of similar trials in other academic libraries using book lease plans. A 1997 follow-up telephone survey of the 14 libraries that responded to Cushman's 1976 survey further illustrates how lease plans fare in academic libraries over time.

The libraries who responded to Cushman's survey show a nearly even split between the two lease plans available at that time: Jostens and Brodart's McNaughton plan. Most of the institutions were junior colleges, small community colleges, or small liberal arts colleges. Satisfaction with the plans was high among these libraries at the time of Cushman's writing. Although some problems with availability of titles appropriate to an academic audience and speed of shipment were noted, the libraries seemed quite happy with many aspects of their lease plans, including user response to their collections as reflected in usage and comments, the low levels of processing and handling required, discounts offered by the vendors, and with the general pleasure of selecting books through the plans.

However, a follow-up telephone survey I conducted in January 1997 revealed that only seven of the 14 libraries Cushman surveyed in 1976 still used lease plans. Of the seven who ceased using lease plans, only two had replaced them with some other means of providing recreational reading materials and one of these relied solely on donated books. Budget problems were the cause of four of the seven cessations; one institution could give no reason for discontinuing the plan because it was stopped so long ago; one institution cited a change in library administration (and therefore agenda) as the reason for ending the lease plan; and one institution moved to a more economical paperback purchase plan after comparing costs, and tracking circulation data and user interests.[9]

In 1997 Brodart's McNaughton Plan appears to be most popular with surveyed academic libraries still using a lease plan. Out of seven who currently use a plan, two are using Baker & Taylor's book leasing system. McNaughton's main competition in 1976, Jostens, was absorbed by McNaughton. Baker & Taylor did not appear on the book lease scene until the mid-1980s. Most of the seven libraries who still use a lease plan report high circulation of the collection, with highest use coming from staff and faculty.

It is impossible to tell what percentage of libraries using book lease plans in 1976 was captured by Cushman's survey. Little more is known about the number of academic libraries currently using plans. Searches on the World Wide Web indicate that some academic libraries are using their Web sites in part to advertise their lease plans; some even include the latest titles and annotations.[10] Representatives at McNaughton and Baker & Taylor report that their plans are often used by academic libraries, but are unable to supply specific data. Further survey research in this area would be very informative.

CREATIVE OPTIONS

Despite thin data, what emerges from even a casual survey of academic libraries that have managed to continue to provide recreational reading materials through the use of book lease plans is a panoply of survival techniques. The special nature of these collections, their visibility and divergent content, require that extra steps be taken to ensure their protection if a library wishes to continue them. Some of the options that are employed to stretch funding, promote high circulation, and garner university support include:

- Seeking funding from Friends groups, student associations, or clubs;
- Considering implementation of very low user fees;
- Housing in a high traffic location;
- Using bookstore display methods (cover out);
- Including in regular library information pamphlets;

- Including in the library Web site;
- Arranging for student newspaper articles on the collection;
- Providing faculty notification service for specific authors or genres;
- Shelving with other current reading materials such as periodicals;
- Finding tie-ins with the curriculum, such as freshman English courses;
- Promoting the collection as a bridge to the public library, not a replacement;
- Using selection input and collection use as an unofficial staff benefit;
- Retitling as the Current or Popular Reading Collection, rather than the Recreational or Leisure Collection.

The academic worth of a popular reading collection, with its high genre fiction and bestseller content, will often be questioned. The service focus of the collection will also be suspect, since many libraries report that their lease plan collection is used more by faculty and staff than by students. Be ready to assert, as Paul Weiner does, that "providing recreational reading for the staff and faculty of a college . . . is an important function of the academic library, if only because it encourages the adults on campus to act as models of library use for the students."[11]

Perhaps the ultimate justification for book lease plans or for popular reading collections in general may be found in the evolving academic library itself. In an era of remote electronic access, libraries may be shifting from places where users must come to find information, to places where they choose to come for discussion and stimulation. Rather than modeling itself as the campus "information barn" of a recent *New Yorker* cartoon, would it not be better for the library to devote at least some resources to providing stimulating links for students, faculty, and staff to the creative worlds embodied in popular fiction and other "recreational" reading materials?

REFERENCES

1. Sturges, Paul and Alison Barr. " 'The Fiction Nuisance' in Nineteenth-Century British Public Libraries." *Journal of Librarianship and Information Science* 24:1 (March 1992), 23-32.

2. Senkevitch, Judith J. and James H. Sweetland. "Evaluating Public Library Adult Fiction: Can We Define a Core Collection?" *RQ* 36:1(Fall 1996), 103.

3. Zauha, Janelle Marie. "Recreational Reading in Academic Browsing Rooms: Resources for Readers' Advisory." *Collection Building* 12:3-4(1993), 58. Since this article, the University of Iowa's browsing room has been dismantled.

4. Information on these lease plans was supplied by the vendors. For further information contact McNaughton (800-233-8467) and Baker & Taylor (800-775-1200) directly.

5. Cushman, Ruth Carol. "Lease Plans: A New Lease on Life for Libraries?" *The Journal of Academic Librarianship* 2:1 (March 1976), 15-19.

6. Cushman, 15.

7. Weiner, Paul B. "Recreational Reading Services in Academic Libraries: An Overview." *Library Acquisitions Practice and Theory* 6:59(1982), 59-70.

8. Data on the MSU-Bozeman McNaughton plan was gathered from the MSU-Bozeman Archives (accession numbers 88006 box 1, 94021 box 1, and 90047), and from librarians Kay Carey and Audrey Jean Haight.

9. Christensen, John O. "Management of Popular Reading Collections." *Collection Management* 6:3-4(Fall/Winter 1984), 75-82.

10. See the University of South Carolina's Web site at http://library.usca.sc.edu/tour/mcnaught.htm and Bradley University's Cullum-Davis Library Web site at http://www.bradley.edu/irt/lib/services/

11. Weiner, 62.

Humanities Collection Librarians
Talk About Their Work

Rebecca Watson-Boone

SUMMARY. Three academic librarians who select humanities titles provide insight into collection work, relations with faculty members, and their sense of "self." The insights of participants in a national study illustrate common and variable elements of this type of library activity. *[Article copies available for a fee from The Haworth Document Delivery Service: 1-800-342-9678. E-mail address: getinfo@haworth.com]*

INTRODUCTION

Over the last 20 years, practitioners and LIS educators have undertaken numerous research studies of humanities scholars.[1] There have been fewer such studies of the librarians who support the scholars. The focus of this article is on academic librarians who select humanities titles. Whether called "selectors," "bibliographers," "collection development (or management) librarians," their actions come at the earliest point in the chain of collection, acquisition, catalog, and reference librarians who are involved with humanities materials and users. The questions that frame the article are (1) what do humanities collection development librarians do, (2) how do they view humanities faculty, and (3) what are some of the characteristics that "define" such librarians?

These questions can be studied in a number of qualitative and quantita-

Rebecca Watson-Boone is President, Center for the Study of Information Professionals, Inc., 4721 West Parkview Drive, Mequon, WI 53092-2136.

[Haworth co-indexing entry note]: "Humanities Collection Librarians Talk About Their Work." Watson-Boone, Rebecca. Co-published simultaneously in *The Acquisitions Librarian* (The Haworth Press, Inc.) No. 19, 1998, pp. 55-67; and: *Fiction Acquisition/Fiction Management: Education and Training* (ed: Georgine N. Olson) The Haworth Press, Inc., 1998, pp. 55-67. Single or multiple copies of this article are available for a fee from The Haworth Document Delivery Service [1-800-342-9678, 9:00 a.m. - 5:00 p.m. (EST)]. E-mail address: getinfo@haworth.com].

tive ways. The material presented here comes from an ongoing national study of librarians in large research libraries. These particular findings are from the 1,000-plus pages of the naturalistic portion of the study–the part that attempts to "capture the natural setting in which [the study] is conducted . . . focus[ing] on the perspective of those involved."[2] Although one-on-one interviews form the basic data collection method, this type of study differs from opinion pieces and individual "how-I-do-it" accounts in the objectivity of its design and execution, and the use of standard data collection and analytical techniques. Beyond the rigor of the research method, naturalistic inquiry succeeds when the personalities that emerge from the findings "create symbols and images that people can connect with, offer figures with whom readers can identify, and ground complex ideas in the everyday realities of organizational life."[3] With this explanation in mind, the author and three pseudonymous librarians consider collection work, revealing along the way some of the characteristics of those who engage in it.

COLLECTION WORK

"Caroline," "Bethany," and "Dan" are from two different, very large, research university library systems. As is increasingly the case across library types, each functions as a boundary-spanner, a "bibliographer with additional responsibilities."[4,5] Dan is the most succinct in describing his work:

> I probably spend half of my time with actual collection development responsibilities, and the other half is personnel matters, reference work, committee work, correspondence, cataloging (what little I do), database searching, [and] everything else. But the greater chunk is collection development.

As the head of a specialized English literature departmental library, he deals with one major language and literature area, and maintains a secondary interest in American literature. Dan has significant personnel and supervisory responsibilities since there is a staff of two librarians, two support personnel, and several student assistants. A typical day includes some time on his own writing, phone calls and consultations with faculty, participation in various committee activities, meetings with his staff, working on newly received approval plan books, studying publishers' brochures and notification slips, and helping at the department's reference desk. With a publisher-based approval plan, Dan finds he does not need to spend too much time with standard English literature topics. "But it is the more ephemeral materials, the trade presses that aren't part of the approval plan, duplicate copies, retrospective collection development–this [is the] type of thing that I spend my time on."

Dan has also been appointed to support colleagues in other specialized collection areas by serving as a group "coordinator." He states of that experience "[I spend] a lot of time just walking around to the other libraries and talking to people, either in formal meetings or informally, just to see what's going on." In addition, there is a monthly meeting with higher level library administrators. With the coordinator position comes a graduate assistant, who allows Dan to continue special projects of value to the collection, the library as a whole, or specific users. Such variety in a single day is welcome, but because of the sheer number of different activities, Dan feels there are many of which he loses track "immediately after doing them." Yet, fundamentally, he believes that "knowing his area [means knowing] as much as [he] can about English . . . And that involves publication and collections, and knowing the demand for that area, which involves the faculty members and graduate students."

Bethany focuses on English and American literature, and includes allied fields such as folklore. In addition, she works with literature translations. To accomplish these tasks, Bethany, however, has no regular staff save for an occasional graduate student assistant. She recently took on responsibility for Italian since no one else was handling it, stating, "I thought we were doing badly at it." This has meant learning the language as well as its literature.

Bethany works closely with English department faculty and graduate students, has taught a university credit library research course at various times, and is active in university-wide faculty committees. She has an established publishing record and is active in several disciplinary associations. A typical day includes "proofreading and revising a list of standing orders and serials, buying materials, working with the faculty, working with the graduate students," and going through a number of reviewing tools, along with new and out-of-print title announcements. She will work on creating finding guides to specialized areas within her collections; may meet with prospective graduate students or faculty; and will resolve reference questions related to her subject areas that are referred from the general reference staff, or that come to her directly from faculty and students for whom she has given bibliographic instruction sessions. She will also find time for meetings with library or university colleagues. But, first and foremost, she says, "I am responsible for the collections."

An example of being "responsible" is found in her decision to handle materials in Italian. Bethany began by learning Italian so she could read the literature. Then the existing collection needed to be assessed so she could develop a profile reflecting areas of coverage, strengths, and limitations. Meetings with Italian department faculty were held to gain a sense of their needs and the direction of the program. Finally, devising a new approval plan included learning what was already on standing order, and developing a cordial working relationship with a key member of an Italian book dealer's staff.

Our third librarian, Caroline, works by herself on four areas: history in a broad, world-wide sense, and German language, literature, linguistics, and culture. Her day includes reviewing new and gift material, assessing the existing collection, making preservation decisions, meeting with faculty and students, holding office hours, and responding to in-depth reference questions having to do with her subject areas. Caroline sees history as a particularly amorphous area: "It's always growing because time is always marching on . . . My colleague who does political science, when the Cold War was declared over, said, 'Well, that's history now'!" Reviewing publishers' announcements and slips, as well as approval plans in her areas, is a daily constant. Since her areas include a language, Caroline finds that when she comes across "an English translation of [a] German novel, I'll check to see if we have this writer in German–because if he's important enough to be getting translated, we should also have the works in German since we have a PhD in German here." She says that even just looking at the approval shelf of recently received materials "can take anywhere from twenty minutes to three hours depending on what turns up there."

One extended responsibility now common to all three librarians is reference work. Indeed, since the mid-1980s, the literature on collection work has found that some amount and kinds of reference and bibliographic instruction have become part of the basic position description for collection librarians.[6] Bunge believes reference work is comprised of information service, instruction in library use, and guidance in the choice of materials.[7] In thinking about reference work, Caroline typifies the three collection librarians:

> By the time [users] are calling me, it's very often not something I can answer in two minutes or off the top of my head . . . It's only a small part of my job description, [but] at certain times, when the students are writing papers, I can spend my whole day on reference questions. Never mind what I was scheduled to do.

For many collection librarians, reference service interactions frequently lead to library/bibliographic "instruction" involvements. Dan, Bethany, and Caroline are not exceptions in these areas either. Each works with classes on either single assignments or a series of sessions. Dan finds his involvement is generally in the "one shot" category, while Bethany frequently teaches between one-third and one-half of a course for graduate literature students. Says Caroline, "I give classes for students who are history majors to tell them how to use library materials. Or I might start up a broader instruction program, you know, in connection with the history department so that the students will get preparation before they're seniors."

Both their core work with collections and their extended responsibilities in areas like reference bring collection librarians into constant contact with humanities faculty. Academic librarians view faculty with a range of attitudes from awe through varying degrees of comfortable collegiality to exasperation.[8] When conducting studies involving faculty, librarians frequently are surprised by unexpected, revealing findings. For example, a Sievert and Sievert study found that philosophy faculty appear to like being asked questions "partly because they have often never been asked or asked themselves these [particular] questions and partly because the questions focus[ed] on their professional commitments and activities."[9] And after interviewing members of a humanities seminar over the course of a semester, Wiberley and Jones concluded that, while humanists largely gain their expertise by reading, "we speculate that because being knowledgeable is fundamental to the academic's sense of self, asking for information [from librarians] can be an unsettling experience."[10]

Bethany, Dan, and Caroline reflect different approaches in how they view and relate to humanities faculty members.[11] Dan sees them basically as users focused on particular fields of interest, who do not need a lot of involvement with librarians. Therefore, his major effort goes into keeping current with what the English department faculty are doing. He believes they see him as a librarian, rather than as a peer. He is comfortable with offering guest lectures in certain courses—"one-shot appearances and that's as far as it goes." Typical of many collection librarians, he receives the departmental newsletter, notices of seminars, spends more informal than formal time with individual faculty, and goes to their holiday parties. He and his staff provide various special services, such as photocopying and distributing tables of contents from various journals. Dan notes he is not personally close to most of the faculty with the exception of one who was hired "about the time that I came here. And I've worked pretty closely with him. He's an aggressive library user, and I appreciate his support and interest. And he does push me to buy as much as I can . . . [W]ith that kind of interest I'm ready to respond with whatever I can do."

Bethany is on the opposite end of the spectrum from Dan. She is very connected with the English department faculty, who, she states, "regard me as one of them." Although not a member of the department, she does have status as a graduate faculty member appointed from the graduate school. When time demands are not too great, she goes over to the department every week: "It was just my plan: I must be here, I must be visible, I must make it easy for people to ask me things. I must attend the colloquium so I know what's going on." When time is stretched, she limits herself to the monthly colloquium and talks with faculty over the phone, by email, or as they come to the library.

Meeting new faculty and working with a new department, such as Italian, are exciting activities for Bethany. One benefit of interviewing new faculty, she feels, is that she learns things about different specialty fields and "about how the library can or cannot support their research." Working now also with the Italian department, she finds, "[has] allowed me to see more clearly how each of the academic departments have their own cultures."

Caroline holds middle ground between her two colleagues and is, perhaps, more typical of collection librarians in general. Over time, she has moved from being in awe to being at home with humanities faculty. When she first began collection work (with a very minimal subject background), she was hesitant to approach them, and it took some time before she "sort of overcame that fear of, 'Oh, I'm not really good enough to do this'. " Luckily, "the faculty were very kind, they were very welcoming, were very happy to have someone from the library coming over and talking to them. They were very willing to tell me what their interests [were] and what their opinions were of the library and how they made use of the library." Now, having taken history courses and spent a number of years in the field, she interacts with them with much greater confidence–routinely and regularly discussing purchases, budget constraints, programmatic changes, bibliographic instruction possibilities, and any number of other things: "[Now] I can dare say to the history department, 'You need to do something better and I can do something in the library to help you do things better'."

Where librarians see their interactions with humanities faculty as basically one-on-one situations, they view both their own relations and those with faculty and students as primarily group situations. In general, they believe both librarians and faculty favor graduate students, who may be described as faculty-in-training and as being very focused on in-depth learning of their specific fields. Caroline expresses a common sentiment when she notes that graduate students are big users of the collection. She and the other librarians, however, keep in touch with "what the undergraduates are reading because we can't buy multiple copies any more the way we used to. So if there's going to be a big crush with assigned readings, I have to know." No student is seen as having the same kind of demands on his/her time as do faculty members, so whereas the librarians typically interact with faculty in a large variety of formal and informal settings, students are seen during predetermined office hours, reference desk times, and class instruction sessions.

All three librarians find faculty colleagues share their commitment to collection areas, frustration over budget constraints that limit acquiring materials needed by faculty and students, and belief in the educational role of libraries. In comparing themselves, their work, and their worldview with that of faculty members, these three collection librarians see themselves as supportive of, but still also independent of, faculty needs. Collection work does mean knowing what faculty members are teaching, researching, and studying; it also means developing a particular subfield of literature "because I think it is important" even when it is not yet actively studied on campus, and selecting a project to engage in because it will result in "something unique that faculty members will not know." If it sounds as though there is a sense of competition at times with faculty, that is because sometimes there is.

A SENSE OF SELF

When librarians talk about goals, satisfactions, and what they try to achieve, they reveal their sense of personal and professional "self." It is part of what social, industrial, and organizational psychologists call a "work identity." Czander describes the process of becoming a particular kind of worker as "the taking of a role." This means that "work for most people involves being in a role, either as an autonomously employed professional or within a large or small corporation. For some, self-realization can be attained by being the best at what one does in one's work, which is the equivalent of being the best within a given role."[12] Braude provides another way of considering the relationship between personality and role:

> Whenever one learns a work role or sets out along a path that may have the semblance of a career, [s/]he confronts the tasks of learning concepts, of assimilating aspects of an entirely new symbol system . . .

And when that person learns to see himself in new ways, such that he can apply new labels to himself and his behavior, he has changed his identity. Who we are . . . is in large measure a function of what we do. Therefore, it is at the social-psychological level, the conceptual or symbolic level, that work and the self meet, that the implications of work performance for the function of the individual are felt at the most personal level.[13]

Caroline, Bethany, and Dan have been collection librarians for an average of ten years. They are comfortable with the work, the library setting, and their various responsibilities. The "fit" between being collection librarians and being themselves has been established.

When talking about what he tries to achieve as a librarian, Dan focuses on his goals as a productive researcher, writer and published author; he wants to know the library's collection in his area as well as be cognizant of and responsive to faculty and student uses and needs as they relate to his department. "In a broad sense anything that I know about English and American literature, anything I learn about it, makes *me* a better reference librarian and a better collection development librarian." When asked to finish a sentence that begins "In my current position as a librarian, I am . . . , " Dan laughs and says, "I am pleased with where I have come and hope that I can develop some of these things further." Among "these things" are increased attention to contemporary poetry, fiction and drama, stronger relations with retiring faculty, and more knowledge about and skill in soliciting money for the department's collection.

Occasionally, Dan feels isolated in his department since he can go for several days without seeing another librarian, due to work arrangements and the physical layout of the library system. This allows him to focus on his collection activities and on his own research, and he knows other librarians are to be found in meetings, within reach of email and the phone, and at campus eateries. He is genuinely happy with what he states as "a good balance between my own interests and my service to the library as a whole." Even when acknowledging the possibility of isolation, he feels–and highly values–the autonomy associated with collection work and with heading a departmental library, noting that "the things I do with the library have almost all been of my own devising. And the way I determine my day is really of my own devising, with the exception of having to go to a given meeting or something." Dan anticipated this kind of environment when he changed universities to move into his current position, and he is pleased that both the library administration and other librarians on campus support each librarian doing his or her own work with minimum constraint and maximum autonomy. For Dan, finding a balanced mixture of institutional involvement and intellectual engagement in his work is very necessary and very comforting.

Bethany ends the "I am . . . " sentence by saying, "I am exhilarated, overworked, intellectually challenged . . . I am feeling incompetent in electronic sources, but I'm looking forward to some workshops that will give me an edge on that. And I know more than most people anyway; I have a Masters Degree in Library Science!" Bethany's sense of achievement is wrapped around "having materials the students and faculty need before they [know] about most of them," and knowing the dimensions, nooks and crannies of her collection areas. With her involvement in disciplinary departments and the larger campus community, she evokes a larger work-world than does Dan. For Bethany, academic libraries have the particular responsibility of being an "independent strength" within their universities, and librarians have the responsibility of adding their own knowledge to the knowledge of campus faculty.

The autonomy of choosing tasks and projects, and when and how she will work on them, allows her to express personal initiative. She is not very happy when administrative policy and procedure, or extended responsibilities, get in the way of collection work. She has, however, found ways to cope with constrained budgets and having her time taken for tasks such as reference work. She muses over, for example, "what a long time it takes to get into being comfortable to make decisions about individual books and to think of a book as it fits into a context of other books, [so] it's ironic that when you have less money it takes more work to spend that money." And she accords value to reference involvement at three specific levels: supporting faculty members, working only with those students who have in-depth reference questions in her collecting areas, and enjoying the intellectual problems associated with times when, as she states, "I can examine some reference materials, compare them to our collection, have some student hands and eyes doing some checking, and put out a guide to our holdings."

The following story illustrates how the satisfaction Bethany feels with her collection work meshes so completely with how she defines herself:

> As I was leaving [lunch], I sat down with a faculty member from English, and he was reading the dissertation of a student writing on Australian literature. This was a great triumph for me, because years ago, a faculty member said, "What are you buying this Australian literature for? Nobody's reading this." And I said, "I'm buying it anyway because I think it's important" . . . To find out that there's a student who's done a dissertation on the collection that I decided to buy–even in the face of opposition from some of my patrons–was extremely gratifying to me last week. There's a dissertation coming

out of here! The teacher didn't know why we could do this. The graduate student didn't know why we could do this. *I* know why we could do this.

As she has done before, Caroline represents a middle ground between the workworld views of Dan and Bethany. Caroline's passion for collection work is now being deliberately tempered by her efforts to balance work with doing some things she likes outside of work, including taking up an instrument and singing. She says, "In my current position in this library I am swamped! . . . I am generally happy to come to work in the morning . . . I am wondering what, very much wondering what it is that I will do next." To Caroline, the future suggests the possibility of "positive growth and change both in the library and personally as a worker." Her goals do not include administration, supervising, or coordinating–although she would love to have an assistant to help with aspects of collection work. All three librarians have experienced such managerial tasks, but for Caroline: "I have sort of come to think that if you want to enjoy your work, that's not the place to be, at least not for me. I really enjoy the hands-on contact with books and with people who read the books, and sort of running it myself; I really do enjoy that." "What I do contributes to the life of the university."

Caroline is happy conducting research and writing, ferreting out new works in any and every format, and building her collection areas. "I like being in charge of my own schedule . . . I can set my own priorities as to when and how I do what." She sees the library's support for autonomy as a "sort of implicit respect that is given to me." Like Bethany, that autonomy is one reason she stays at her library.

Caroline is part of a multi-member collection unit that has a common central area but individual, personal offices. "Maybe some people who go into bibliography . . . enjoy working alone. Even though I enjoy being autonomous, I really like having colleagues close at hand that you can talk to and interact with." Caroline likes problem solving and making things happen within her collection. Working with faculty and students provides for interesting days and meaningful work.

CONCLUSION

Caroline, Bethany, and Dan's thoughts and concerns provide insight into our three questions of what do collection librarians do, how do they view humanities faculty, and what are some of the characteristics that "define" them as librarians. The three share strong positive feelings about the value of their work. Each approaches collection librarianship with different intensity, relates variably to faculty, and expresses goals and satisfactions through uniquely personal frameworks.

They share a similar variety of tasks in their work lives. The range of tasks will be familiar to generalist librarians in libraries with smaller collections or staff size. Librarians who have added collection work to their overall jobs because of budget and staff reductions, changes in organizational arrangements, or the trend toward involving increasing numbers of librarians in direct public service activities will also recognize the array of tasks.[14]

Most librarians can find their own views represented somewhere in Bethany, Caroline, and Dan's range of involvement in and beliefs about humanities faculty members. Size of institution and traditions regarding faculty involvement in collection activities are among the elements that make a difference in relations between librarians and humanities faculty. For most librarians who do any collection work, there is shared understanding that faculty tend to see librarians as vitally important service providers rather than as peers.[15]

The socio-psychological "characteristics" of goals and satisfactions are the most personal of the three areas. Do Caroline, Dan, and Bethany express beliefs and attitudes that are commonly held by most collection librarians? They do reflect a number of the profile characteristics that emerge from findings of national studies of librarians who took the Strong Interest Inventory, the ACT Interest Inventory, and/or the Myers-Briggs Type Indicator vocational interest tests: they are intelligent, thoughtful, self-sufficient, and interested in a life of the mind. They show imagination, decisiveness, self-respect, and leadership qualities.[16] The three collection librarians are not immune from frustration or feelings of stress. They fret about inadequate budgets and especially about anything that takes them away from their primary work on collections. But none seems to exhibit the kind of "work alienation" that Nauratil describes.[17] And each reflects positively on being a librarian. In a number of ways, then, Bethany, Dan, and Caroline are like many librarians. They like what they do, believe their own particular work is the best work a library offers and, at the end of the day, are content to come back tomorrow and work on it some more.

REFERENCES

1. Stone, Sue. 1982. "Humanities Scholars: Information Needs and Uses." *Journal of Documentation* 38/4 (Dec.):292-313; Watson-Boone, Rebecca. 1994. "The Information Needs and Habits of Humanities Scholars." *RQ* 34/2 (Win.): 203-216.

2. Mellon, Constance Ann. 1990. *Naturalistic Inquiry for Library Science: Methods and Applications for Research, Evaluation, and Teaching.* Contributions in Librarianship and Information Sciences. New York: Greenwood Press. pp. 2-3.

3. Lightfoot, Sara Lawrence. 1983. "Afterword: The Passion of Portraiture" from *The Good High School*, as reprinted in *Qualitative Research in Higher Education: Experiencing Alternative Perspectives and Approaches*, edited by Clifton Conrad, Anna Neumann, Jennifer Grant Haworth, and Patricia Scott. 1993. Needham Heights, MA: Ginn Press. p. 402.

4. pseudonyms to protect confidentiality.

5. Allison, Terry L. and Marion T. Reid. 1994. "The Professionalization of Acquisitions and Collection Development." Chapter 2 in *Recruiting, Educating, and Training Librarians for Collection Development*, edited by Peggy Johnson and Sheila S. Intner. New Directions in Information Management, no. 33. Westport, CT: Greenwood Press.

6. Haskell, John D., Jr. 1984. "Subject Bibliographers in Academic Libraries: An Historical and Descriptive Review." *Advances in Library Administration and Organization* 3:73-84; Keller, Michael A. 1994. "Late Awakenings: Recruiting Subject Specialists to Librarianship and Collection Development." In Chapter 4 in *Recruiting, Educating, and Training Librarians for Collection Development*, edited by Peggy Johnson and Sheila S. Intner.

7. Bunge, Charles. 1980. "Reference Services." In *ALA World Encyclopedia of Library and Information Services*. 1st ed. Chicago: American Library Association.

8. See for example, Hall, H. Palmer and Caroline Byrd. 1990. *The Librarian in the University: Essays on Membership in the Academic Community*. Metuchen, NJ: The Scarecrow Press, Inc.; Smith, Eldred. 1990. *The Librarian, The Scholar, and the Future of the Research Library*. New York: Greenwood Press; and Engeldinger, Eugene A. 1992. "Frustration Management in a Course-Integrated Bibliographic Instruction Program." *RQ* 32/1:20-24.

9. Sievert, Donald and MaryEllen Sievert. 1989. "Philosophical Research: Report from the Field." In *Humanists at Work: Disciplinary Perspectives and Personal Reflections*. Chicago: University of Illinois at Chicago, Institute for the Humanities and the University Library. p. 81.

10. Wiberley, Stephen and William Jones. 1989. "Patterns of Information Seeking in the Humanities." *College & Research Libraries* 50/6 (Nov.):640.

11. Guest, Susan. 1987. "The Use of Bibliographic Tools by Humanities Faculty at the State University of New York at Albany." *Reference Librarian* 18:157-72; Nissenbaum, Stephen. 1989. "The Month Before 'The Night Before Christmas.' " In *Humanists at Work*; and Curley, Edwin M. 1989. "Comments on 'Philosophical Research: Report from the Field.' " In *Humanists at Work*.

12. Czander, William M. 1993. *The Psychodynamics of Work and Organizations: Theory and Application*. New York: Guilford Press. p. 294.

13. Braude, Lee. 1983. *Work and Workers: A Sociological Analysis*. Malabar, FL: Robert E. Krieger Publishing Co. p. 166.

14. Cubberley, Carol W. 1987. "Organization for Collection Development in Medium-Sized Academic Libraries." *Library Acquisitions: Practice & Theory* 11/4:297-323.

15. For a general discussion of the small library situation, see Jones, Jr., Plummer Alston and Connie L. Keller. 1993. "From Budget Allocation to Collection Development: A System for the Small College Library." *Library Acquisitions: Practice & Theory* 17/2:183-189.

16. Scherdin, Mary Jane, ed. 1994. *Discovering Librarians: Profiles of a Profession*. Chicago: American Library Association, Association for College and Research Libraries.

17. Nauratil, Marcia J. 1989. *The Alienated Librarian*. New Directions in Information Management, Nr. 20. New York: Greenwood Press.

Censored, Forbidden and Underground Czech Novelists: A Selective Review

Debora Richey

SUMMARY. Severe Communist repression from the 1960s to 1989 forced many of Czechoslovakia's major novelists to emigrate to foreign countries, where several continued to produce impressive fictional works. Those novelists who remained in their homeland were forced to either submit their novels for state censorship prior to official publication or to circulate their manuscripts through underground means. Despite continued crackdowns, banned and censored novelists produced not only some of Czechoslovakia's greatest literature, but many world class novels as well. This article identifies major Czech novelists from this period and their works, as well as anthologies, full-length critical studies and background resources. *[Article copies available for a fee from The Haworth Document Delivery Service: 1-800-342-9678. E-mail address: getinfo@haworth.com]*

With the possible exception of the period between the two world wars, which saw the emergence of such literary giants as Karel Capek, Vladislav Vancura and Jaroslav Hasek, the Czech novel has achieved during the past thirty years a richness and variety unparalled in the history of Czechoslovakian literature. In its venerable thousand year history, Czech literature has never known such an outpouring of talent, with writers producing not

Debora Richey is Bibliographer/Reference Librarian, California State University Fullerton Library, Reference Section, P.O. Box 4150, Fullerton, CA 92834.

[Haworth co-indexing entry note]: "Censored, Forbidden and Underground Czech Novelists: A Selective Review." Richey, Debora. Co-published simultaneously in *The Acquisitions Librarian* (The Haworth Press, Inc.) No. 19, 1998, pp. 69-91; and: *Fiction Acquisition/Fiction Management: Education and Training* (ed: Georgine N. Olson) The Haworth Press, Inc., 1998, pp. 69-91. Single or multiple copies of this article are available for a fee from The Haworth Document Delivery Service [1-800-342-9678, 9:00 a.m. - 5:00 p.m. (EST)]. E-mail address: getinfo@haworth.com].

69

only magnificent Czech fiction, but some of the finest prose of the twentieth century. What is even more remarkable about this fictional output is that it was achieved during a period of severe repression and censorship.

The roots of this boom extend back to the late 1950s and early 1960s when a more politically and artistically relaxed Communist Party allowed new developments in fiction in conjunction with the "New Wave" in Czech film propelled by the release of *Closely Watched Trains*, winner of the 1967 Academy Award for Best Foreign Language Film. Novelists during this relatively relaxed period–Ladislav Fuks, Bohumil Hrabal, Milan Kundera, Vladimir Paral, Josef Skvorecky, Ludvik Vaculik, etc.–were permitted to publish innovative novels that challenged the literary and political status quo. These young authors, most of whom were born in the 1920s, were also allowed to develop and mature as writers.

Developments peaked in 1968 with the short-lived Prague Spring, a period which saw the abolishment of censorship and unprecedented political and artistic freedom. This all too brief moment of freedom came to an end in August 1968 when armies of the Warsaw Pact led by the Soviet Union army invaded Czechoslovakia. Official firings and purges began in October 1969. Had the Prague Spring not come to a sudden and abrupt end, Czech novelists could have attained instant international recognition for their fictional works. Instead, a situation was created almost without precedence: nearly all of Czechoslovakia's finest writers were expelled from all normal publishing channels and forced to go underground with their writings. Besides losing all possibility of publishing their works in their country, writers lost their jobs at universities, publishing houses, newspapers and journals. Many took menial jobs to survive.

As a result of this crackdown, novelists were reduced to three options: (1) exile; (2) permanent status as a "banned" writer permitted only to circulate works in typed copies; or (3) status as an "official" writer subject to state or self-censorship. A number of Czechoslovakia's best novelists– Ota Filip, Jiri Grusa, Milan Kundera, Arnost Lustig, Josef Skvorecky, etc.–chose exile. Unlike many emigre writers who lose their voices once they leave their homeland (Solzhenitsyn, for example), exiled Czech writers continued to write novels in their native language, creating some of their best-known fiction. Other writers, notably Ivan Klima and Ludvik Vaculik, found it impossible to leave their country and to give up their artistic freedom, turning instead to underground methods of distributing their writings. These courageous writers faced imprisonment and persecution by the police. "Official" novelists whose works were apolitical in nature and therefore less likely to attract the interest of censors (Ladislav Fuks, Vladimir Paral, Jiri Sotola) were allowed to write provided that they or the state exercised censorship over their novels. These writers, however, soon found out that cooperation did not guarantee publication. The new post-occupation regime published one or two of their books, but the bulk of their works remained suppressed. On occasion, writers would "repent" and swear allegiance to the system, but these public apologies never really helped.

The primary goal of the Czech puppet regime was to silence writers. Czechoslovakians have always had a tremendous respect for writers and the Prague Spring would not have been possible without the determined efforts of the Czech Writers' Union. When the crackdowns began, writers were given harsh prison sentences and there were well-publicized show trials (Vaclav Havel's case, for instance), but for the most part, the Party's goal was to strip writers of their traditional influence. Mass terror was replaced by rigid forms of control. The government encouraged or forced emigration, knowing that once abroad, the influence of active dissident writers would be blunted. Those that stayed were treated to daily persecution and molestation by the police, and were deliberately cut off from all normal literary, political and publishing opportunities. Publication through "official" channels required that writers submit their works to authorized government censors who usually butchered their writings. Some novels were so zealously censored that they became almost unrecognizable to their authors.

The result was that Czechoslovakia developed two types of literature: the first, an official literature written for political manipulation with the Party's blessing but not read; and a second, a clandestine literature disseminated in typed and carbon-duplicated copies, and sold through personal contact for a price covering the cost of production. These underground works, known as *samizdats*, were eagerly read and shared. The Communist government controlled photocopiers as well as printing presses, and the distribution of uncensored photocopied texts was punishable by law. Carbon copy reproductions, however, were legal, although in practice they could incur strong official displeasure.

Samizdat editions of banned novels were published in the 1950s and 1960s, but novelists resorted to these carbon-duplicated copies in increasing numbers from 1970 to 1989. Forbidden novelists began to exchange their manuscripts in 1969 at meetings in Ivan Klima's apartment. Ludvik Vaculik then took over as general editor of the documents, establishing a "publishing" enterprise called Edice Petlice (Padlock Books), which included by the 1980s close to 400 titles.[1] Soon other clandestine book enterprises sprang up, as well as hundreds of samizdat periodicals. Some books in Czech were smuggled out to the West to be published, then smuggled back in to be distributed in samizdat editions. Other samizdat novels were smuggled out and published by Sixty-Eight Publishers, the Toronto-based firm established by Skvorecky and his wife to assist Czech authors. For the most part, though, these novels were ignored by Western publishers.

During this period there was also renewed interest in *feuilletons*. The ideal genre for samizdat publications, feuilletons are brief creative pieces which generally run two-and-a-half to four typewritten pages in length (between 1500 and 2000 words). These short literary pieces, which covered all topics, gave authors the feeling of having their works published. Writers could also stay in touch with their readers through these brief works while working on longer projects. On occasion, novelists would loosely string together a collection of feuilletons to form a full-length fictional work.

Until recently, many of the novelists from this period remained largely inaccessible, except to a Czech–and, to some extent, European–readership. Gradually, though, these once suppressed novels are being published in the Czech and Slovak republics, and increasingly these innovative works are being translated into English. The following article is a brief survey of Czech novelists during these decades of artistic repression. The purpose is not to list every banned Czech novelist and their works for the past thirty years, but to identify instead the major novelists and novels produced during this period. While there are lists of banned Czech and Slovak writers, there is actually no bibliography of the thousands of fictional works published in samizdat editions.[2] Because university libraries, especially those with declining book budgets, can no longer collect everything, novelists and works that have been singled out for especially high critical praise are identified with an asterisk(*).

What needs to be emphasized is that these authors are not only remarkable Czech novelists, but world class fiction writers as well. Each of these writers had a unique experience with the Communist regime during this period, and these experiences are reflected in their writings and publishing opportunities. Many of the novels listed (*The Republic of Whores*, *Love and Garbage*, *The Year of the Frog*, etc.) were originally samizdat publications, and as translations of these once-banned works continue, many more should be available in English language editions.

Pricing information and ISBN numbers are provided for titles currently listed in *Books in Print*. Only novelists whose works have been translated into the English language are included. Unless otherwise stated, Czech or Czechoslovakia refers to the three regions (Bohemia, Moravia, Slovakia) which made up Czechoslovakia until the Velvet Divorce in 1993 split the country into two separate nations: the Czech Republic and the Republic of Slovakia.

CENSORED OR FORBIDDEN WRITERS IN CZECHOSLOVAKIA

Ladislav Fuks (1923-1994)

One of Czechoslovakia's most important writers, Fuks studied philosophy, psychology and art history, taking his doctorate at Prague University. His first novel, *Dr. Theodore Mundstock* (1963), was an overnight sensation and established his reputation in Czechoslovakia and abroad. A prolific writer, Fuks went on to produce collections of short stories and a dozen novels. He was working on his memoirs at the time of his death. To appease the censors, Fuks in the 1970s turned to fantasy and the "socialist realism" preferred by the Party (e.g., *The Mice of Natalia Mooshaber*, *Return from the Rye-Field*), but these attempts were poorly received, embarrassing, and obviously written without conviction. He returned to his early style and existential themes in the 1980s.

Heavily influenced by Kafka, Fuks' best novels feature the grotesque and bizarre, and are primarily concerned with the theme of death. *Dr. Theodore Mundstock* tells the story of a Jewish clerk in occupied Prague who tries to prepare for his removal to a concentration camp. *The Cremator* (1967) describes the career of an undertaker who puts to death his partly Jewish wife and children, then serves as an operator in a Nazi death camp.

Fiction

Mr. Theodore Mundstock. New York: Four Walls Eight Windows, 1991. ISBN 0-941423-62-X. $10.95.
The Cremator. Trans. by E. M. Kandler. New York: Marion Boyars, 1985. ISBN 0-7145-2808-0. $14.95.

Jiri Grusa (1938-)

A poet, literary critic and translator as well as a novelist, Grusa was one of the founding fathers of the literary journals *Ivar* and *Sesity*. Although government authorities quietly tolerated samizdat publications, especially those which did not openly challenge the Communist system, Grusa was jailed in 1978 for circulating nineteen samizdat copies of his novel *The Questionnaire* and for announcing that he intended to publish the book abroad. In 1981, the authorities asked him to emigrate, and once out of the country he was stripped of his citizenship and barred from reentry. He then took up residency in West Germany. Most recently he has served as the Czech ambassador to Germany.

An unlikely work to be deemed subversive by the censors, *The Questionnaire* is not the usual indictment of Communism. In this fanciful novel, the main character has applied for fifteen jobs since being placed on a list of political undesirables. While filling out his sixteenth application, designed to determine his political reliability, he uses the personal data required on the form to reflect on his boyhood, parents, family history, past loves, and home town. *The Questionnaire* is the only Grusa novel available in English, but his other works have been translated into numerous languages.

Fiction

The Questionnaire, or, Prayer for a Town and a Friend. Trans. by Peter Kussi. New York: Farrar, Straus & Giroux, 1982. Published simultaneously in Canada by McGraw-Hill Ryerson, Ltd., Toronto.

**Bohumil Hrabal (1914-)*

The son of a brewer, Hrabal held a series of jobs–salesman, foundry worker, paper salvage worker, stagehand, etc.–before settling down to full-time writing in 1963 at the age of forty-eight. This delay in choosing a career made Hrabal older and more experienced than most of his fellow novelists. He shot to international fame in the 1960s with *Closely Watched Trains*, a coming-of-age novel set during the Nazi occupation of East Europe. The novel (later made into a celebrated film) was a ground-breaking work that helped to free Czech literature from the strictures of state-approved socialist realism. After the Soviet invasion, Hrabal's works were confiscated and burned, and his name was added to the list of banned authors. For the next eight years, Hrabal's works were published underground.

Long regarded as Czechoslovakia's greatest living writer, Hrabal's daring brilliancy and unpredictability as a writer, combined with his tremendous popularity, made Czech authorities nervous. The censors were also suspicious of Hrabal's disinterest in politics. In the mid-1970s, government authorities approached the author, offering to resume official publication of his works in exchange for a public "self-criticism." In a controversial move, Hrabal agreed to this arrangement and recanted his former dissident activities on state television. After his "rehabilitation," the state began to publish his once banned books, but in severely censored editions. His parable on state censorship, *Too Loud a Solitude*, for instance, was published only after long offending passages were eliminated and tenses changed to indicate that events in the novel took place long before the Communists seized power in 1948. This censorship and Hrabal's public confession, however, failed to diminish his popularity. His first state-published novel, the semi-fictional *Postriziny* (translated as *The Haircutting* or *Cutting It Short*) was an instant hit. All 20,000 printed copies of the book sold out in less than two hours.

Thereafter, Hrabal published his novels and short stories in two editions: one in expurgated state-sanctioned editions; the other in unexpurgated and complete samizdat editions. This double distribution of Hrabal's works infuriated the state-owned publishing houses and the police, but the authorities never apprehended his samizdat distributors. It was only after the fall of Communism that Hrabal's samizdat publisher, Vaclav Kadlec, admitted that he was able to elude the police by using state-owned machines to type and copy the author's books. Kadlec also played a major part in smuggling Hrabal's novels out for publication abroad.[3]

Hrabal's works are difficult to categorize. Chaplinesque in style, they combine the humorous with the poignant, and often feature members of the working class. His short stories and novels are deceptively simple, masking complex themes and plotlines written with great skill. In *Dancing Lessons for the Advanced in Age*, an old shoemaker relates his rambling life story. One long unbroken sentence, the novella is a parody of the last chapter of James Joyce's *Ulysses*. *Too Loud a Solitude*, a satire on Czech disinformation campaigns, describes the life of a paper baler who compresses old books into scrap paper. *The Death of Dr. Baltisberger* is a collection of stories based upon tales told in the beer halls of Prague.

Hrabal has written over eighty works translated into twenty-three languages, but so far only a handful have been translated into English. In 1995, the Czech PEN Club and the Czech Writers' Community nominated the author for the Nobel Prize for literature. Noted Hungarian writer Peter Esterhasy has also written a playful homage to the author entitled *The Book of Hrabal* (Northwestern University Press, 1994). In this unusual and inventive novel, the main character, a pregnant woman contemplating abortion, composes imaginary letters to the Czech writer.

Fiction

*Closely Watched Trains. Foreword by Joseph Skvorecky. Trans. by Edith
Pargeter. Evanston, IL: Northwestern University Press, 1995. ISBN
0-8101-1278-7. $12.95. ISBN 0-8101-0857-7. $9.95 pbk.
*Dancing Lessons for the Advanced in Age. Trans. by Michael H. Heim.
New York: Harcourt Brace, 1995. ISBN 0-15-123810-3. $14.00. ISBN
0-15-600232-9. $7.95 pbk.
*The Death of Dr. Baltisberger. Trans. by Kaca Polackova. Garden City,
NY: Doubleday, 1975.
*I Served the King of England. Trans. by Paul Wilson. New York: Random
House, 1990. ISBN 0-679-72786-8. $12.00 pbk.
*The Little Town Where Time Stood Still and Cutting It Short. Intro. by
Joseph Skvorecky. Trans. by James Naughton. New York: Pantheon
Books, 1993. ISBN 0-679-42225-0. $23.00.
*Too Loud a Solitude. Trans. by Michael H. Heim. New York: Harcourt
Brace, 1990. ISBN 0-15-190491-X. $17.95. ISBN 0-15-690458-6.
$9.00 pbk.

**Ivan Klima (1931-)*

Born in Prague, Klima was transported in 1941, at the age of ten, to the
concentration camp of Terezin, where he was lucky enough to survive for
four years until the arrival of the victorious Russian army. He began
publishing works in the 1950s and worked on the staff of Prague's famous
literary journal, *Literarni listy*. A visiting professor at the University of
Michigan at the time of the Soviet invasion of Czechoslovakia, Klima
elected to return to his country. After his return, Klima's apartment became a gathering place for young Czech writers to read from their unpublished works. His return to Czechoslovakia and his dissident activities,
however, cost him dearly. He was forced to take a series of menial or odd
jobs–courier, train driver, archaeologist, book smuggler, surveyor's assistant–described in his collection of stories *My Golden Trades*. His books
could not be officially published in Czechoslovakia so they circulated
underground in samizdat editions. Many of his works, though, were
smuggled out and published abroad. The majority of his audience in the
1970s and 1980s were foreigners who read him in translation, but this
international exposure established Klima as one of the most admired writers of the postwar generation. Since 1989, Klima's works have been published in the United States, with a number of them making the *New York
Times* best seller list.
    A writer of enormous power and originality, Klima is noted for his

light, ironic and eloquent prose. His major works–*Love and Garbage, Judge on Trial, Waiting for the Dark, Waiting for the Light*–are novels of conscience that mix the political and personal while tracing the demeaning history of Communism in Czechoslovakia. Despite the often sad and depressing content of his fiction, Klima's works are noted for their hopeful and optimistic tone. Most recently, Klima has written on the positive and negative effects of the fall of Communism on Czech artists and culture.[4]

Fiction

*Judge on Trial. Trans. by A. G. Brain. New York: Random House, 1994. ISBN 0-679-73756-1. $14.00 pbk.
*Love and Garbage. Trans. by Ewald Osers. New York: Vintage International, 1993. ISBN 0-679-73755-3. $11.00 pbk.
My First Loves. Trans. by Ewald Osers. New York: W. W. Norton, 1989. ISBN 0-393-30601-1. $9.95 pbk. A collection of interconnected stories, this is Klima's first work to be published in the United States.
*My Golden Trades. Trans. by Paul Wilson. New York: Scribners, 1994. ISBN 0-684-19727-8. $22.00.
My Merry Mornings. Trans. by George Theiner. New York: Readers International, 1984. ISBN 0-0523-04-0. $14.95. ISBN 0-930523-05-9. $11.95.
A Ship Named Hope: Two Novels. Trans. by Edith Pargeter. London: Gollancz, 1970.
A Summer Affair. Trans. by Ewald Osers. London: Chatto & Windus, 1987.
*Waiting for the Dark, Waiting for the Light. New York: Grove Press, 1995. ISBN 0-8021-1574-8. $21.00.

Nonfiction

The Spirit of Prague. Trans. by Paul Wilson. London: Granta, 1994. ISBN 0-9645611-2-3. $10.05 pbk. A collection of critical pieces, including feuilletons, an interview with Philip Roth, an autobiographical sketch about Klima's boyhood and beginnings as a writer, and musings on literature and life.

**Milan Kundera (1929-)*

The most celebrated Czech novelist from this era, Kundera is greatly admired for his stylish, elegant novels which have placed him in the forefront of twentieth century novelists. After studying literature, music and film, Kundera accepted a professorship at the Prague Film Institute. He tried his hand at a number of genres–poetry, short stories, journalism, literary history–before producing his first novel, *The Joke*, in 1965. *The Joke* was an instant bestseller in his homeland, and when translated and published abroad, the novel established Kundera's international reputation. After the 1969 purges, Kundera was fired from his faculty position, and his books were confiscated and banned and all copies removed from Czech libraries. For the next five years, the author held a series of odd jobs (including horoscope writing), but was largely supported by his wife's earnings as a private English-language instructor. Through the efforts of his French friends, Kundera was invited to lecture at the University of Rennes in France in 1975. Four years later, the Czech government deprived him of his citizenship, and on the initiative of President Mitterand, he became a French citizen in 1981. Kundera then moved permanently to Paris, publishing a handful of novels and two collections of critical essays on the art of fiction, and his work evolved in new experimental directions. He continued to write his novels in Czech but wrote his essays in French.

Over the past twenty years, Kundera has established himself as the best known Czech writer since Kafka. He has had, however, a testy and tenuous relationship with the Czech dissident literary community, many of whom have openly criticized him for failing to publicly stand up against Communism. Like many Czechs, Kundera in his youth was a member of the Communist Party and wrote pro-Communist/Stanlinist verse. He later was removed from the Party and participated actively in the Prague Spring, but did not become an emigre spokesman for his homeland after leaving Czechoslovakia. Copies of Kundera's novels smuggled into Czechoslovakia were criticized for their misrepresentation and trivialization of Communist repression. Literary critics such as the influential Milan Jungmann pointed out Kundera's false picture of life under neo-Stalinist rule. In *The Unbearable Lightness of Being*, for instance, the main character, Tomas, would not have been legally allowed to quit his profession as a surgeon and take up window cleaning. Jungmann, who actually worked as a window cleaner after the purges, is also quick to point out that Tomas would have been too tired after a day of exhausting work to participate in sexual escapades in the evenings. Sensitive to these criticisms, Kundera has never made an official return visit to his homeland and has been slow to publish his novels in Czechoslovakia. Kundera has also chosen to write his latest novel, *Slowness*, in French, a move which symbolizes to many Czechs a further retreat by the author from his homeland.

Highly popular and highly admired, the novels of Kundera are polished, theoretical and cerebral. His first novels–*The Joke* and *Life Is Elsewhere*– are traditionally structured, but his most recent fiction is experimental and more loosely arranged. His books combine cynicism with humanism, autobiography with fiction, and witty satire with philosophical discourse. Two of his books–*The Book of Laughter and Forgetting* and *The Unbearable Lightness of Being*–attempt to combine erotic fiction with events from Czech history. His collections of critical essays concentrate on the novel as an art form.

Kundera's novels are greatly admired by literary critics, and, as a result, he has received extensive critical attention. Two journals–*Salmagundi* (no. 73, Winter 1987) and the *Review of Contemporary Fiction* (Summer 1989) have devoted entire issues to discussions of Kundera's works. Kundera has received numerous literary awards and been nominated for the Nobel Prize for literature.

Fiction

The Book of Laughter and Forgetting: A Novel. Trans. by Michael Henry Heim. New York: HarperCollins, 1996. ISBN 0-06-092608-2. $12.00 pbk. A French translation was also completed by Aaron Asher.
The Farewell Party. Trans. by Peter Kussi. New York: Viking Penguin, 1987. ISBN 0-14-009694-9. $11.95 pbk.
The Joke: Definitive Version. New York: HarperCollins, 1993. ISBN 0-06-099505-X. $13.00 pbk.
Immortality. Trans. by Peter Kussi. New York: HarperCollins, 1992. ISBN 0-06-097448-6. $13.00 pbk.
Laughable Loves. New York: Viking Penguin, 1988. ISBN 0-14-009691-4. $11.95.
Life Is Elsewhere. Trans. by Peter Kussi. New York: Viking Penguin, 1986. ISBN 0-14-006470-2. $11.95 pbk.
Slowness: A Novel. Trans. from the French by Linda Asher. New York: HarperCollins, 1996. ISBN 0- 06-017369-6. $21.00.
The Unbearable Lightness of Being. Trans. by Michael Henry Heim. New York: HarperCollins, 1988. ISBN 0-06-091465-3. $13.00 pbk.

Nonfiction

The Art of the Novel. Trans. from the French by Linda Asher. New York: HarperCollins, 1989. ISBN 0-06-097204-1. $10.00 pbk.
Testaments Betrayed: An Essay in Nine Parts. Trans. from the French by Linda Asher. New York: HarperCollins, 1995. ISBN 0-06-017145-6. $24.00. ISBN 0-06-092751-8. $13.00 pbk.

Bibliographies, Criticism/Interpretation

Banerjee, Maria N. *Terminal Paradox: The Novels of Milan Kundera.* New York: Grove Press, 1991. ISBN 0-8021-3233-3. $12.95 pbk.

Brand, Glen. *Milan Kundera: An Annotated Bibliography.* New York: Garland, 1988.

*Milan Kundera and the Art of Fiction: Critical Essays. Ed. by Aron Ajii. New York: Garland, 1992. ISBN 0-8153-0038-7. $60.00. A collection of critical essays, half of which have been previously published.

Misurella, Fred. *Understanding Milan Kundera: Public Events, Private Affairs.* Columbia, SC: University of South Carolina Press, 1992. ISBN 0-87249-853-0. $29.95. An undergraduate guide to Kundera's fiction and non-fiction.

O'Brien, John. *Milan Kundera and Feminism: Dangerous Intersections.* New York: St. Martin's Press, 1995.

Porter, Robert C. *Milan Kundera: A Voice from Central Europe.* Aarhus, Denmark: Arkana Publishers, 1981.

Arnost Lustig (1926-)

After the German occupation of Czechoslovakia, Lustig and his family were rounded up and sent to Terezin, a Czech concentration camp. He and his family were then transferred to Auschwitz, where several members of his family (including his father) were killed, and from there to Buchenwald. In March 1945, he jumped off a deportation train for liquidation in Dachau and returned to Prague to join the Czech resistance. At the end of the war, Lustig became a writer, broadcaster and screenwriter, but after the Russian invasion he fled to Yugoslavia. Lustig, who was a prominent writer in Czechoslovakia at the time of the invasion, was then declared an enemy of the state and his published books were confiscated and destroyed. He eventually moved to Washington, D.C. where he taught writing, literature, and film at American University.

Despite his exile, Lustig has maintained his creative output, publishing numerous short stories and novels, most of which reflect the traumatic experiences of Jewish life under Nazi occupation and in concentration camps. *Night and Hope,* his first work to be translated into English, is a collection of short stories detailing life in Terezin; *Darkness Casts No Shadow* is the story of two young boys who briefly escape during a train wreck on their way from one concentration camp to another; and *The Unloved,* a fictional diary, describes the life of an adolescent prostitute in a concentration camp. Many of the characters in his fiction are children, frequently adolescent girls. Lustig's prose is sparse and unsentimental, and despite the horrors described, noted for its tone of hope and optimism. *A Prayer for Katerina Horovitzova* was nominated for the National Book Award in 1974, and two of his novels–*Dita Saxova* and *The Unloved*–won the Jewish National Book Award. Lustig still writes in Czech and now translates his works into English.

Fiction

Children of the Holocaust. Evanston, IL: Northwestern University Press, 1995. Includes *Night and Hope, Diamonds of the Night* and *Darkness Casts No Shadow.*
Darkness Casts No Shadow. Trans. by Jeanne Nemcova. Washington, DC: Inscape, 1976.
Diamonds of the Night. Trans. by Jeanne Nemcova. Evanston, IL: Northwestern University Press, 1986. ISBN 0-8101-0706-6. $15.95 pbk.
Dita Saxova. Trans. by Jeanne Nemcova. Evanston, IL: Northwestern University Press, 1994. ISBN 0-8101-1131-4. $49.95. ISBN 0-8101-1132-2. $17.95 pbk.
Indecent Dreams. Evanston, IL: Northwestern University Press, 1990. ISBN 0-8101-0909-3. $9.95 pbk. A collection of short stories.
Night and Hope. Trans. by George Theiner. Evanston, IL: Northwestern University Press, 1985. ISBN 0-8101-0702-3. $9.95 pbk. A collection of short stories.
A Prayer for Katerina Horovitzova. Trans. by Jeanne Nemcova. Woodstock, NY: Overlook Press, 1987. ISBN 0-87951-998-3. $15.95. ISBN 0-87951-223-7. $9.95 pbk.
Street of Lost Brothers. Evanston, IL: Northwestern University Press, 1990. ISBN 0-8101-0959-X. $32.95. ISBN 0-8101-0960-3. $12.95 pbk. A collection of short stories.
The Unloved: From the Diary of Perla S: A Novel. Evanston, IL: Northwestern University Press, 1996. ISBN 0-8101-1347-3. $12.95 pbk.

Vladimir Paral (1932-)

A chemical engineer who worked for years in a textile factory before turning to full-time writing, Paral was a major influence on Czech fiction in the 1960s and 1970s. His scientific background accounts for the strong role that science and technology play in his works. While other Czech writers, such as Skvorecky and Kundera, were able to achieve worldwide fame in exile, Paral is an example of a novelist who remained in his homeland while trying to stay out of the way of the Communist censors.

During the 1960s he published a series of novels–*Trade Fair of Fulfilled Desires*, *Private Gales*, and *Lovers and Killers* (literary puns of works by Thackeray, Noel Coward and D. H. Lawrence, respectively)–which were immensely popular. His third novel and the first to be translated into English, *Catapult*, was issued at the height of the Prague Spring and declared a masterpiece by critics and his fellow countrymen. The novel went on to make best seller lists throughout Europe. Many of his novels describe the Czech state of mind before and during the Prague Spring. After the Communist clampdown, Paral continued to write and remained one of Czechoslovakia's most popular writers, but because his books were not translated and published abroad, he lacks the wide readership he deserves. Recently, though, Catbird Press has published English language translations of his third novel, *Catapult* (1967), and his fifth novel, *The Four Sonyas* (1971). In the 1980s, Paral turned to writing science fiction.

Although Paral tried to write without inciting the interest of the censors, his works frequently are burlesques and subtle parodies of Eastern European socialism. A stock character in his witty and farcical novels is the bored, lazy managerial technocrat who has lost all interest in Marxist ideology. In *Catapult*, Jacek Jost, a bored husband and chemical engineer, advertises in a lonely hearts magazine for companionship, winding up with seven mistresses in seven different towns. With an engineer's attention to detail, Jost calculates how long it takes to travel from one town to the other, moving from woman to woman, but always unable to make a choice between them. In the picaresque *Four Sonyas*, the lovely heroine who has four sides to her personality, attracts every repulsive man who sees her as she waits for the ideal man to whisk her away.

Fiction

Catapult: A Timetable of Rail, Sea, and Air Ways to Paradise. Trans. by William Harkins. Highland Park, NJ: Catbird Press, 1989. ISBN 0-945774-04-4. $15.95. ISBN 0-945774-17-6. $10.95 pbk.
The Four Sonyas. Trans. by William Harkins. Highland Park, NJ: Catbird Press, 1993. ISBN 0-945774-15-X. $22.95.

Martin M. Simecka (1957-)

Martin Simecka is the son of well-known writer and dissident, Milan Simecka (1930-1990), who was imprisoned and not allowed to publish after the Soviet invasion of Czechoslovakia in 1968. Because of his father's political activities, the young Simecka was denied university admission, turning instead to a series of menial jobs. He currently runs a publishing house, Archa, which issues once banned books.

Although both his parents are Czech, Simecka has chosen to write in Slovak, and his first novel, *The Year of the Frog*, is the first Slovak language novel to be published in the United States in the 1990s. In 1992, *The Year of the Frog* won the Pegasus Prize for Literature after a jury selected it as the best novel written in Czechoslovakia in the preceding ten years, and later picked up the *Los Angeles Times* Book Prize for a first published work in any language. Set in Bratislava in the early 1980s and highly autobiographical, the novel describes the coming of age of Milan, a young former track star forced to take menial jobs because of his father's dissident activities. The attention and praise given to this first novel, which was first issued in samizdat installments in the 1980s, had made Simecka an author to watch.

Fiction

The Year of the Frog. Trans. by Peter Petro. Baton Rouge, LA: Louisiana State University Press, 1993. ISBN 0-8071-1869-9. $22.95.

Josef Skvorecky (1924-)

A virtuoso of modern Czech, Skvorecky has been active in various genres: poetry, novels, filmscripts, literary/film criticism, short stories, detective fiction, etc. He began publishing books in the 1950s but had immediate problems with the repressive Communist regime, which censored or banned most of his works and later confiscated his unsold works. After losing his editorial post at a Czech journal, Skvorecky found it increasingly difficult to obtain official work and turned to translating and publishing his work under other authors' names. After the Soviet-led Warsaw Pact invasion of Czechoslovakia in 1968, he fled to Toronto where he taught at the University of Toronto. When he left his homeland, Skvorecky already had a formidable reputation, and the subsequent translation and publication of his banned novels, plus the publication of new works, have only added to his luster. Although he still writes his fiction in Czech, he is considered a Canadian writer.

Along with his wife, Skvorecky in 1972 established Sixty-Eight Publishers, the premier publishing house of Czech literature in the West over the past few decades. Sixty-Eight Publishers has issued books by many noted Czech writers (e.g., Milan Kundera, Vaclav Havel, etc.) and smuggled editions of works both in and out of Czechoslovakia.

A jazz aficionado (he plays the saxophone), Skvorecky is noted for his open-ended improvisational writing style. His most internationally successful works are his cycle of autobiographical novels focused on his alter ego, Danny Smircky. Told through the eyes of his autobiographical surrogate, these primarily first-person narratives—*The Cowards* (1958), *The Republic of Whores* (1971), *The Miracle Game* (1972), *The Swell Season* (1974), *The Engineer of Human Souls* (1977), and *The Bass Saxophone* (1979)–parallel Skvorecky's experiences of Nazism, Communism and Canadian exile. An admirer of American detective fiction, he has also branched out into the mystery/detective genre (*Miss Silver's Past*) and created the character of a Czech policeman, Lieutenant Boruvka, featured in a number of novels (*Sins for Father Knox, The End of Lieutenant Boruvka, The Mournful Demeanor of Lieutenant Boruvka, The Return of Lieutenant Boruvka*). Although basically a comic and anti-political writer, Skvorecky has also recently produced historical fiction, publishing *The Bride of Texas* (1996), an epic novel on Czech immigrant soldiers under General Sherman in the Civil War, and *Dvorak in Love* (1984), a biographical novel of the great Bohemian composer. Classical music lovers and critics consider *Dvorak in Love* to be "possibly the finest fictional treatment of the life of any composer."[5]

Because Skvorecky's works have been available in the West since the 1960s, he is one of the few contemporary Czech writers to be featured in full-length critical studies. *World Literature Today* (Autumn 1980) devoted an entire issue to discussion of Skvorecky's work.

Fiction

The Bass Saxophone. Trans. by Kaca Polackova Henley. New York, NY: Ecco Press, 1994. ISBN 0-88001-370-2. $12.00 pbk.

**The Bride of Texas.* Trans. by Kaca Polackova Henley. New York, NY: Alfred A. Knopf, 1996. ISBN 0-679-44411-4. $27.00.

**The Cowards.* Trans. by Jeanne Nemcova. New York, NY: Ecco Press, 1980. ISBN 0-912946-75-X. $8.95 pbk.

**Dvorak in Love: A Light-hearted Dream.* Trans. by Paul Wilson. New York, NY: Alfred A. Knopf, 1987. ISBN 0-317-58073-6. $18.95. ISBN 0-393-30548-1. $10.00 pbk.

The End of Lieutenant Boruvka. Trans. by Paul Wilson. New York, NY: Norton, 1990.

**Engineer of Human Souls: An Entertainment on the Old Themes of Life, Women, Fate, Dreams, the Working Class, Secret Agents, Love and Death.* Trans. by Paul Wilson. New York: Knopf, 1984. ISBN 0-394-50500-X. $17.95.

The Miracle Game. Trans. by Paul Wilson. New York, NY: Norton, 1992. ISBN 0-393-30849-9. $10.95 pbk.

Miss Silver's Past. Intro. by Graham Greene. Trans. by Peter Kussi. New York, NY: Ecco Press, 1985. ISBN 0-88001-074-6. $7.50 pbk.

Mournful Demeanor of Lieutenant Boruvka: Detective Tales. New York, NY: Norton, 1991. ISBN 0-393-30786-7. $8.95 pbk.

Republic of Whores: A Fragment from the Time of Cults. Trans. by Paul Wilson. New York, NY: Ecco Press, 1994. ISBN 0-88001-371-0. $21.00. ISBN 0-88001-428-8. $15.00 pbk.

The Return of Lieutenant Boruvka: A Reactionary Tale of Crime and Detection. New York, NY: Norton, 1991. ISBN 0-393-02928-X. $18.95.

Sins for Father Knox. New York, NY: Norton, 1991. ISBN 0-393-30787-5. $8.95 pbk.

The Swell Season: A Text on the Important Things in Life. Trans. by Paul Wilson. New York, NY: Ecco Press, 1986. ISBN 0-88001-090-8. $8.50 pbk.

The Tenor Saxophonist's Story. New York, NY: Ecco Press, 1977. ISBN 0-88001-461-X. $23.00. A collection of ten interconnecting tales.

Nonfiction

Headed for the Blues: A Memoir. Trans. by Kaca Polackova Henley. New York, NY: Ecco Press, 1996. ISBN 0-88001-462-8. $23.00.

Talkin' Moscow Blues: Essays about Literature, Politics, Movies, and Jazz. New York, NY: Ecco Press, 1988. A collection of the best essays and reviews by Skvorecky published since leaving Czechoslovakia.

Bibliographies, Criticism/Interpretation

Kalish, Jana. *Josef Skvorecky: A Checklist.* Toronto: University of Toronto Library, 1986. An extensive bibliography of primary and secondary sources, including translations, anthologies, interviews, articles, reviews, etc.

*Solecki, Sam, ed. *The Achievement of Josef Skvorecky.* Toronto: University of Toronto Press, 1994. The first collection in any language to be devoted to Skvorecky's works.

Solecki, Sam. *Prague Blues: The Fiction of Josef Skvorecky, a Critical Study.* Toronto: ECW Press, 1990.

*Trensky, Paul I. *The Fiction of Josef Skvorecky.* New York: St. Martin's Press, 1991. A basic undergraduate critical guide to Skvorecky's major literary works.

Ludvik Vaculik (1926-)

A Moravian, Vaculik began publishing his works in 1960 while also serving on the editorial board of Czechoslovakia's main cultural weekly, *Literarni noviny.* An outspoken, active dissident, he achieved instant notoriety in 1968 with his populist manifesto "Two Thousand Words" urging Czechs to challenge the existing Communist power structure. The manifesto became one of the main pretexts for the Soviet engineered invasion and led to his systematic persecution for the next twenty years. Vaculik never spent long periods in prison but was subjected to various forms of ill-treatment: he was expelled from the Communist Party and lost his job; the secret police harassed his family, bugged his telephone, camped outside his residence, and banned his children from attending higher education; and he and his wife, both healthy, were forced to visit a venereal disease clinic. Offered an exit permit as an alternative to a trial, he refused. After Vaculik established Padlock Books, a samizdat enterprise, he was regularly interrogated in hourly, weekly or monthly installments about contributing authors and works. These interrogations are described in *A Cup of Coffee with My Interrogators*, a collection of loosely-related feuilletons.

Because Vaculik's writings were outlawed, his novels were first published abroad in Czech. He was instrumental in establishing the feuilleton as a popular medium for banned writers and he is considered the master of this short format. His fiction is highly autobiographical, and, as would be expected, deals often with the theme of human rights. *The Guinea Pigs*, a political parable, describes experiments conducted by a bank clerk on pet guinea pigs. The book received the first George Orwell Prize awarded by Penguin Press for literature commenting on contemporary social problems. Vaculik remains an important voice in Czech literature, but like many of his colleagues, the bulk of his work remains untranslated and unavailable in the West.

Fiction

The Axe. Trans. by Marion Sling. Evanston, IL: Northwestern University Press, 1994. ISBN 0-8101-1018-0. $12.95 pbk.

The Guinea Pigs. Trans. by Kaca Polackova. Evanston, IL: Northwestern University Press, 1986. ISBN 0-8101-0726-0. $12.95 pbk.

Nonfiction

A Cup of Coffee with My Interrogators: The Prague Chronicles of Ludvik Vaculik. Intro. by Vaclav Havel. Trans. by George Theiner. London: Readers

International, 1987. ISBN 0-930523-34-2. $14.95. ISBN 0-930523-35-0. $7.95 pbk.

OTHER CZECH WRITERS

In addition to the authors discussed, there are other notable but little-known novelists from this period whose works remain largely inaccessible to the general Czech reading public. With the reemergence of a free press, many of their works are now being published through normal channels for the first time in the Czech and Slovak Republics and English-language translations are anticipated as well. Although there are no hard statistics, literary historians estimate that of the hundreds of banned and forbidden writers during this period about half were silenced completely, unable to circulate their works even in samizdat editions.

Overlooked Czech and Slovak novelists from this period who deserve attention and readership include Alexandr Kliment (1929-), Jiri Kratochvil (1940-), Eda Kriseova (1940-), Lenka Prochazkova (1951-), Jiri Sotola (1924-), the author of allegorical fiction, and Slovak Dominik Tatarka (1913-89). There are also a handful of significant novelists–notably Jan Benes (1936-), Jiri Mucha (1915-1991) and Karel Pecka (1928-)–who were incarcerated in the 1950s and 1960s, and whose works primarily focus on prison and concentration camp life. Imprisoned in 1981-82, Eva Kanturkova (1930-) has focused on imprisonment from a female perspective (e.g., *My Companions in the Bleak House*). In addition, there are still other exiled writers–Ota Filip (1930-), Jiri Hochman (1926-), Pavel Kohout (1928-), Vera Linhartova (1938-), Jan Vladislav (1923-), etc.–who have not received the critical attention given to other emigre writers. Linhartova, who now writes in French and whose works are unavailable in English language translations, is often considered the most genuinely original woman writer from this period. Most of these writers have produced works in other genres as well.

Writers active both before and after the Russian occupation were followed by a younger set of fiction writers. These writers, born primarily after 1959, had to deal with the stifling atmosphere of the 1970s and 1980s. Many of these novelists are stylistically and thematically different from the postwar generation of writers. While their works address the Czech-Russian conflict, many have tried to branch out into more personal and independent directions. This post-occupation set of writers includes Zuzana Brabcova (1959-), Jachym Topol (1962-), and Michal Viewegh (1962-). Since 1989, a handful of young Czech novelists have created fictional works which have received warm critical attention from American critics, including Martin Vopenka (*Ballad of Descent*), Iva Pekarkova (*Truck Stop Rainbows*, *The World Is Round*), and Libuse Monikova (*The Facade: M.N.O.P.Q.*), who writes in German.

ANTHOLOGIES

Although somewhat limited in scope, the following anthologies provide a good cross selection from the works of Czechoslovakia's best fiction writers.

Description of a Struggle: The Vintage Book of Contemporary Eastern European Writing. Ed. by Michael March. Intro. by Ivan Klima. New York: Vintage Books, 1994. ISBN 0-679-74514-9. $14.00.
*Good-Bye, Samizdat: Twenty Years of Czechoslovak Underground Writing. Ed. by Marketa Goetz-Stankiewicz. Evanston, IL: Northwestern University Press, 1992. ISBN 0-8101-1010-5. $42.95. ISBN 0-8101-1035-0. $19.95 pbk.
New Writing in Czechoslovakia. Ed. by George Theiner. Middlesex, England: Penguin, 1969. A collection of poetry and short stories published since 1962, including contributions from Milan Kundera and Josef Skrovecky.
*This Side of Reality: Modern Czech Writing. Ed. by Alexandra Bucher. London: Serpent's Tail, 1996. ISBN 1-85242-378-1. $13.99.
*The Writing on the Wall: An Anthology of Contemporary Czech Literature. Ed. by Antonin Liehm and Peter Kussi. New York, NY: Karz-Cohl Publishing, Inc., 1983. Many of the pieces here were reprinted in *Hour of Hope: An Almanac of Czech Literature 1968-1978* (Toronto: Sixty-Eight Publishers, 1978).

BACKGROUND INFORMATION AND LITERARY CRITICISM: FULL-LENGTH WORKS AND ESSAY COLLECTIONS

The following full-length studies will provide historical and background information on Czech-Russian literary relations, as well as secondary criticism on the works of Czech authors. So far, only a handful of critical studies on Czech literature during this period have been produced.

Cross Currents 3: A Yearbook of Central European Culture. Ed. by Ladislav Matejka and Benjamin Stolz. Ann Arbor, MI: University of Michigan, 1984.

Czech Literature Since 1956: A Symposium. Ed. by William E. Harkins and Paul I. Trensky. New York: Bohemica, 1980. Includes critical essays on Bohumil Hrabal, Milan Kundera, Vladimir Paral and Ludvik Vaculik.

Fiction and Drama in Eastern and Southeastern Europe: Evolution and Experiment in the Postwar Period: Proceedings of the 1978 UCLA Conference. Ed by Henrik Birnbaum and Thomas Eekman. UCLA Slavic Studies, vol. 1. Columbus, OH: Slavica Publishers, Inc., 1980.

French, A. *Czech Writers and Politics, 1945-1969.* New York: Columbia University Press, 1982.

*Hamsik, Dusan. *Writers Against Rulers.* Trans. by D. Orpington. New York, NY: Random House, 1971.

*Hruby, Peter. *Daydreams and Nightmares: Czech Communist and Ex-Communist Literature, 1917-1989.* East European Monographs, no. 290. New York: Columbia University Press, 1990. ISBN 0-88033-187-9. $38.00.

_____. *Fools and Heroes: The Changing Role of Communist Intellectuals in Czechoslovakia.* Oxford: Pergamon Press, 1980. ISBN 0-08-024276-6. $127.00. ISBN 0-08-026790-4. $100.00 pbk.

Kusin, Vladimir V. *The Intellectual Origins of the Prague Spring: The Development of Reformist Ideas in Czechoslovakia, 1956-1967.* London: Cambridge University Press, 1971.

Literature and Politics in Central Europe: Studies in Honour of Marketa Goetz-Stankiewicz. Ed. by Leslie Miller. Columbia, SC: Camden House, 1993. ISBN 1-879751-68-2. $59.95. Includes contributions by Ivan Klima and Josef Skvorecky, as well as a study of samizdat publications.

Modern Slovak Prose: Fiction Since 1954. Ed. by Robert B. Pynsent. London: Macmillan, 1990.

Novak, Arne. *Czech Literature.* Ed. with a Supp. by William E. Harkins. Trans. by Peter Kussi. Ann Arbor, MI: Michigan Slavic Publications, 1986. The Supplement covers 1946 to 1985.

Petro, Peter. *A History of Slovak Literature.* Montreal: McGill-Queens University Press, 1995. ISBN 0-7735-1311-6. $44.95.

Skilling, H. Gordon. *Samizdat and an Independent Society in Central and Eastern Europe.* Columbus, OH: Ohio University Press, 1989. ISBN 0-8142-0487-2. $45.00.

Souckova, Milada. *A Literary Satellite: Czechoslovak-Russian Literary Relations.* Chicago, IL: University of Chicago Press, 1970. ISBN 0-226-76840-6. $12.50.

BIBLIOGRAPHIES, REVIEW SOURCES AND PUBLISHERS

Once Czech authors were blacklisted, publishers could not only no longer publish their works, but it was also forbidden to mention their names or works in any print source, not even in scholarly journals or dissertations. This blacklist coupled with a booming undocumented underground literature has made it difficult to chronicle samizdat publications. Only a few bibliographical surveys of the samizdat fictional works of authors have been completed and compilations of the works of Czechoslovakia's novelists are not yet available.

In a positive move, the Czech National Library recently began issuing its national bibliographies–*Ceska narodni bibliografie: Knihy, disertace, periodika, clanky/Czech National Bibliography: Books, Journal Articles, Periodicals, Dissertations*–in both paper and CD-ROM versions.[6] These initial bibliographies have focused on state-approved publications, but the listings are expected to include parallel literature as well.

So far, English language editions of either official or underground Czech or Slovak novels have concentrated on the most important and influential authors and works. This trend is expected to continue, and researchers and readers should have no trouble finding review literature. Nearly all of these impressive novels have been issued by established publishers and university presses, and reviews are readily available through standard review sources (e.g., *Library Journal*, *Kirkus*, *New York Review of Books*, etc.).

Czechoslovakia has a long rich tradition of translations, and the quality of Czech translations is excellent. Many translators and critics consider Paul Wilson, who himself was expelled from Czechoslovakia, the best translator of Czech literature.

CONCLUSION

When reviewing and critiquing the literature from this period, there is a tendency to emphasize the political plight of these authors rather than the literature. Ivan Klima and other Czech novelists have been alternately angered and bemused by the tendency of Western journalists to ask "What are you going to write about now?" Patronizing reporters wrongly assume that with the fall of Communism these writers have nothing to write about in the absence of an enemy. Nothing could be further from the truth. While unpublished works by these writers are expected to be published abroad during the next few years, it should be remembered that these novelists have continued to write and there is the promise of continued fresh creative work as well.

REFERENCES

1. Vaculik described his experience with Padlock Books in an article ("A Padlock for the Castle") written for the *Index on Censorship*, March 1989: 31-33. This brief article is also included in *ACTA*, no. 3 and 4 as an introduction to the Petice bibliography.

2. A partial bibliography of Petice publications ("Padlock Books, 1973-1987") will be found in *ACTA: Quarterly of the Documentation Centre for the Promotion of Independent Czechoslovak Literature*, no. 3 and 4, 1987: 38-108. For a brief time, Vaculik worked with a librarian, Zdena Erteltova, who possessed a professional impulse to establish a card index and maintain a bibliography, but because of sudden police raids and the threat of confiscation, it was actually preferable not to carefully document samizdat publications.

3. Herbert Mitgang, "The Czech Literati: Too Old to Be New, but New Nevertheless," *New York Times*, January 7, 1991, sec. C: 11.

4. See "Progress in Prague," *Granta*, no. 47 (Spring 1994): 249-255.

5. Jim Svejda, *The Record Shelf Guide to the Classical Repertoire*, 3rd ed. (Rocklin, CA: Prima Publishing, 1992).

6. Available from: Albertina icome Praha; Revolucni 13; Praha 1, 110000 Czech Republic.

De(construction) of Literary Theory:
The Rise of Anti-Theory Fiction

Mona Kratzert
Debora Richey

SUMMARY. Over the past two decades a bewildering array of new methodologies and critical approaches to literature have sprung up. This boom in the number of critical theories, coupled with the excesses of theorists, have left librarians, students and academicians confused and disoriented. Creative individuals–novelists, dramatists, faculty members, etc.– have responded by producing fictional works that criticize, satirize or parody these new critical approaches. This article identifies representational works in this growing subgenre and points out the perceived excesses that are being criticized or satirized. *[Article copies available for a fee from The Haworth Document Delivery Service: 1-800-342-9678. E-mail address: getinfo@haworth.com]*

Tremendous interest has been shown in expanding the literary canon to include more theoretical approaches, as well as more women and ethnic and cultural groups previously excluded from literary studies. Over the past two decades there has been a bewildering array of new methodologies and critical approaches to literature: deconstruction, gender studies, new historicism, cultural materialism, postcolonial studies, composition studies, feminist studies, etc. At the same time, accepted critical theories–New

Mona Kratzert and Debora Richey are Bibliographers/Reference Librarians, California State University Fullerton Library, P.O. Box 4150, Fullerton, CA 92834.

[Haworth co-indexing entry note]: "De(construction) of Literary Theory: The Rise of Anti-Theory Fiction." Kratzert, Mona, and Debora Richey. Co-published simultaneously in *The Acquisitions Librarian* (The Haworth Press, Inc.) No. 19, 1998, pp. 93-111; and: *Fiction Acquisition/Fiction Management: Education and Training* (ed: Georgine N. Olson) The Haworth Press, Inc., 1998, pp. 93-111. Single or multiple copies of this article are available for a fee from The Haworth Document Delivery Service [1-800-342-9678, 9:00 a.m. - 5:00 p.m. (EST)]. E-mail address: getinfo@haworth.com].

Criticism, Marxist criticism and reader-response theory, etc.–have been challenged, forcing academicians and critics to examine and reexamine their critical paradigms. One long-established historical field, Renaissance Studies, is even under pressure to update and change its name to Renaissance and Early Modern Studies. What's "in" and what's "out" seems to change from day to day: celebrated theories that only a few scholars understood are abruptly pronounced dead, and new, even more opaque theories are touted as more perceptive and reasonable.

These new theoretical and methodological orientations have disoriented librarians, students and professors alike. Librarians often find it difficult to keep up with the ever-growing number of theories, while shrinking material budgets hinder the purchase of the hundreds of books and new journals issued each year devoted to new paradigms. Under pressure to keep up with the growing number of critical approaches, literature professors complain that students are no longer interested in the whole picture, concerned more with becoming theoretical sophisticates rather than well educated. The pretensions of literary criticism seem to pose a threat to humanist education, and several conservative critics–Allen Bloom, George F. Will and Lynn Cheney in particular–see these new theories as devaluing what they consider to be the greatness of Western Civilization.

Students, in turn, often perceive themselves as victims of scholarly attempts to expand the canon, forced to read barely comprehensible texts at the expense of older, more traditional works. Instead of reading, discussing and researching works, students are now expected to decode and decipher "coherent texts," and adopt an obscure critical vocabulary that uses such truncated concepts as "transhistorical forces," "marginalized subjects" and "transgressive discourses." It is not unusual for a college or university student to sit through an entire quarter or semester course and find instructors reducing and interpreting all the works on the reading list to one narrowly focused literary theory.

To counteract this growing focus on critical theory at the expense of literature itself, many creative individuals–critics, novelists, playwrights, academicians, and even students–have responded in the way they know best: by producing fictional works that criticize, satirize or parody these new critical approaches. The array of fictional anti-theory books has been dazzling.[1] Writers have produced novels, plays, comics, mock biographies and mysteries, all with the express purpose of lampooning theorists and theories. Many writers, notably Malcolm Bradbury and Charles Palliser, have been able to parody the frequently impenetrable and obfuscated terminology of theorists by mimicking or reproducing their language in mock formats. In many cases, writers have co-opted and/or incorporated literary theory with fiction to create a form of "critifiction" or "theorifiction" in which literary theories become the source of the storyline. In these works, readers are presented with a number of post-structuralist narratives or texts, which they are then invited or expected to analyze critically, as the author makes fun of the actual process of deconstruction.

This is not to say, though, that professionals in the literary field view critical theory as an unnecessary or useless approach to literature. Indeed, nearly all would view criticism and the interpretation of works as an accepted component of literary studies. What is being criticized and satirized are the perceived excesses of members of the theoretical coterie. As the job market has become tighter and pressure to publish or perish has increased, faculty members and critics are producing papers and articles geared to an increasingly small number of other theorists, creating a literature for professionals only. Many of the topics discussed are perceived as unintendly hilarious. A list of some of the papers presented at recent Modern Language Association (MLA) Conferences, for example, provides ample fuel for critics who believe literary scholarship has been taken over by popular culture, political correctness, and multiculturalism: "Abusive Furniture: Das Ding"; "Ads as Texts: Using Popular Media in College Writing Courses"; "Bambi on Top"; "Dandyism and Dieting: The Camp Performance of Richard Simmons"; "From Slave Ship to Cruise Ship: Repetition and Difference in a Caribbean Context"; " 'I Never Ate a White Man Yet': The Poetics of Indigestion"; "An Investigation into the Distribution of the Adverb Simply in Modern British English"; "Kleist and Amphibian Sexuality"; "Like a Virgin: Ruskin's Medea as Madonna"; "The Resisting Monkey: *Curious George*, Slave Narratives, and Postcolonial Theory"; "The Sentimental Culture of the Internet: E-mail and Epistolary Etiquette."[2]

Many of the program presentations are so loony they appear to be self-parody, and do much to support the popular perception of the conference as an annual literary "Gong Show." For many fiction writers, the Modern Language Association and its annual meeting, with its own politically correct jargon, etiquette and cliques, represent a perfect target, and a number of satirical works in this subgenre (e.g., *Murder at the MLA*, *Mustang Sally*, *Small World*) use the conference as a setting. Anti-MLA sentiment has grown so strong in recent years that a new scholarly group, the Association of Literary Scholars and Critics, has been formed to counteract the excesses of MLA.[3]

Along with the anti-theory and anti-MLA bents of these works, there is also the strong theme of the university as a jungle with academics pitted against each other and embroiled in absurdist academic governance.

Traditionalists struggle against radical upstarts, often with nefarious results, as both argue about what works should or should not be included in the literary canon. The plots in these works increasingly involve the stalking or murdering of English faculty members by their fellow colleagues (e.g., *Book: A Novel, Murder at the MLA*, etc.).

The purpose of this article is not to identify all anti-theory works of fiction, but to identify some of the best and most representational titles in this growing area of literature. Since this subgenre is so new and developing, annotations have been included to provide a sense of the contents, themes, narrative techniques and textual schemata used by authors. Much of this fiction is as avant-garde as the theories themselves and their catchy titles do not adequately represent their content. Because the trend toward theoretical analysis of literary works shows no sign of abatement, books in this mushrooming subgenre should continue to be regularly published. What the books in this core collection have in common are cleverness, inventiveness and accessibility—traits that make them delightful to read, and certainly at odds with the hundreds of serious theoretical tomes published each year.

Pricing information and ISBN numbers are provided for titles currently listed in *Books in Print*.

INDIVIDUAL AUTHORS AND WORKS

Edward Allen

Mustang Sally. New York: W. W. Norton and Company, 1992. ISBN 0-393-03403-8. $19.95.

Recently divorced, second-rate English Professor Packard Schmidt hangs out at strip joints near the campus of Amherst College in Indiana and frequents Las Vegas on gambling junkets. On one trip, at the request of a colleague, he searches for one of his former students, now working at a bordello called the Mustang Valley Inn. After employing her services, Schmidt is forced to resign when the affair is discovered. Desperately seeking new employment, he heads for the MLA annual convention where he agrees to serve as a panelist on a program titled "The Leukemic Muse of Literary Eroticism: Is Sex Dead or Just Immune-Suppressed?" To enliven his presentation and prove his worth as a critic, Schmidt brings along his hooker friends to the program, where, not unexpectedly, a riot breaks out.

Malcolm Bradbury

Doctor Criminale. New York: Penguin Books, 1993. ISBN 0-14-023167-6. $11.00.

Eating People Is Wrong. Chicago, IL: Academy Chicago Publishers, 1991. ISBN 0-89733-189-3. $6.95.

My Strange Quest for Mensonge. New York: Penguin Books, 1988. ISBN 0-14-010706-1. $6.95.

A critic, parodist, film and television screenwriter, frequent talk show guest, and satirical novelist, Malcolm Bradbury is, along with writer Angus Wilson, also known as the co-founder of a celebrated creative writing course taught at the University of East Anglia. Bradbury has produced many works of literary criticism, as well as numerous satiric academic novels. Literary theory and theorists are frequent topics in his novels, but three of his works–*Eating People Is Wrong* (1959), *My Strange Quest for Mensonge* (1988) and *Dr. Criminale* (1992)–are particularly noted for their satiric attacks and take-offs on criticism.

Set in a provincial "red-brick" British university, *Eating People Is Wrong* describes the antics of a group of eccentric students and faculty. The book's main character, Professor Stuart Treece, a befuddled liberal humanist, is modeled on critic F. R. Leavis. First written in 1959 and considered a minor classic, this comic novel is very much a work of the 1950s, and Bradbury himself in the Afterword admits that it is a light, "generous comedy" he would have trouble writing in the 1990s. This social satire does, however, contain a number of features that reappear in later anti-theory satires: the growing trend to produce articles and dissertations on oddball topics (in one case, fish imagery in Shakespeare's history plays); the humanist professor besieged by "new movements" he is unable or unwilling to understand; and the brusque, self-seeking American professor/critic willing to espouse any avant-garde theory.

Written in a style and tone reminiscent of Derrida and Foucault, *My Strange Quest for Mensonge* is a critique of the great French literary critic Henri Mensonge, the Deconstructionist's Deconstructionist, who may or may not exist. Mensonge (French for lie) has taken the deconstructionist's view of the absence of the author from his works to heart by completely disappearing: "Mensonge has gone further, insisting that he was never even there in the first place, has never been known to anyone, even his closest friends, that he is no one, has achieved nothing, and does not exist. In short he has claimed to be a totally absent absence" (p. 26). Mensonge's major critical work, *La Fornication Comme Acte Culturel*

(Fornication as a Cultural Act) has also never been read by anyone, but the absence of any actual writing by him only testifies to its universality. Much of this mock biography's humor comes from the inside jokes. The 8:25 Geneva to Paris Express, for instance, which provided Saussure with an example of the distinction between "langue" and "parole," forever changes the life of Mensonge, whose absence is explained by his failure to catch this train, mistaking it for another, thereby contradicting Saussure's theory. In addition, Bradbury deconstructs the book's index, filling it with blind cross-references, and includes a bibliography of real and imagined works. Bradbury also satirizes the inclination of critics and the public alike to confuse him with novelist David Lodge by naming David Lodge as the translator of *My Strange Quest*.

In *Dr. Criminale*, journalist Francis Jay is hired by a television production company to research the famous philosopher-critic-writer Bazlo Criminale, who, in his youth, quarrelled with Heidegger, disputed with Adorno, and argued against Lukacs. Criminale, a composite of various theorists, including Barthes, Derrida, de Man and even David Lodge's Maurice Zapp, spends his time moving from conference to conference where he is photographed with everyone from Umberto Eco to Arnold Schwarzenegger to Pol Pot. As Jay pursues Criminale from city to city, he gradually discovers that the philosopher is a shady intellectual con artist.

Christine Brooke-Rose

Textermination: A Novel. New York: New Directions, 1991. ISBN 0-8112-1230-0. $21.95. ISBN 0-8112-1216-5. $10.95 pkb.

Christine Brooke-Rose is known to a narrow, elite audience for novels that play games with narrative techniques, ideas and language. Dense and multi-layered, *Textermination* is set in San Francisco at a sort of literary convention—the Annual Convention of Prayer for Being. Gathered here are Emma Woodhouse, Emma Bovary, Lotte (Goethe's and Thomas Mann's), Mr. Elton, Lancelot, Boule de Suif, Dorothea Brooke, the Alices (huge and tiny), Gilgamesh, Gregor Samsa (as beetle), and most other fictional characters to hear papers about themselves (e.g., "Interpreting the Soldier from Achilles to *Catch 22*") and to attend Rituals for Being where prayers are offered for their continued existence in the minds of the Creator/Reader. According to the fashion of the time some characters have more existence than others. To check on their status, characters continually consult the Canon to determine if they have been dropped and thus terminated. During the course of the novel major characters are tossed out of the Canon and disappear, resulting in a change of the narrative voice. But their greatest problem is that reading is disappearing. Those characters who have the good fortune to be read at all are brutally analyzed by teachers, scholars and students into schemata, psychic movements, social significances, etc.

A. S. Byatt

Possession: A Romance. New York: Random House, 1990. ISBN 0-394-58623-9. $22.95.

Possession, a Booker-award winning novel, breaks out of the confines of campus fiction and, complete with melodrama, converges upon both romance and quest. Roland Mitchell, a research assistant editing the works of Victorian poet R. H. Ash, is a dullish traditionalist while Maud Bailey, a university professor studying Victorian writer Christabel LaMotte, is an ardent feminist critic. The two contemporary scholars discover previously unimagined evidence of a brief illicit love affair between their two Victorian subjects and "possessed" by their find, covertly try to reconstruct the affair and its enigmatic aftermath. A complex plot involves Mitchell and Bailey and a bevy of rival professors in a race for this information and for newly uncovered documents and manuscripts. The rival professors include two ugly Americans (stock characters in this type of fiction) who seek the information for their own academic self-promotion.

Byatt ingeniously juxtaposes the previous century with the world of contemporary academia. There are long sections of "original" correspondence between Ash and LaMotte, extracts from their poetry and from journals kept by Ash's wife, LaMotte's companion, and others. There are also satiric commentaries by critics on the poets and their works. Byatt's method of narrating her twin tales allows presentation of the story from many points of view which, in turn, reveals the unreliability of apparent truth or the impossibility of only one interpretation. The novel's ironic title, as multilayered as the text, refers to the paradox of possessing truth, the rightful possession of literary texts, the possession of the researcher's soul by the researched author, and the possession of one person by another.

Frederick C. Crews

The Pooh Perplex; A Freshman Casebook. New York: Dutton, 1963.

The Pooh Perplex, a parody in the style of the undergraduate student casebook, is an early work of this subgenre. Essays in this anthology of mock explication written by fictitious scholars are hilarious travesties of contemporary literary critics or schools. Since this work is now over thirty years old, it does not include structuralist, post-structuralist, and deconstruction critical approaches. Each author applies his own elaborate exegetical technique to A. A. Milne's *Winnie the Pooh* in order to discover the true meaning of the text, and each essay deliberately contradicts the others. Author names, brief biographies, and study questions which follow chapters are also the quintessence of academic goofiness. Crews, a Berkeley English professor, demonstrates familiarity with excesses both in refereed literary journals and in university English curriculum.

The *Pooh Perplex* also spawned two other Pooh take-offs: Benjamin Hoff's *The Tao of Pooh* and John Tyerman Williams' *Pooh and the Philosophers*.

Patricia Duncker

Hallucinating Foucault. 2nd ed. New York, NY: Ecco Press, 1997. ISBN 0-614-16317-X. $19.00.

Duncker, a literary critic and Foucault specialist, has loosely based *Hallucinating Foucault* on Herve Builbert's *To the Friend Who Did Not Save My Life*, a fictionalized account of his real affair with Foucault. More serious than other works discussed, the novel is both a mystery and romance, interweaving several themes which have occupied literary critics of various schools. The novel presents the experience of lived theory, with characters and storyline appearing as embodiments of complex literary theories and ideas, and examines the singular relationship between reader and writer. The narrator, a graduate student, sets out on a passionate quest to discover the truth behind the theoretical texts of Paul Michel, who, housed in a mental institution, emerges as a fleshed-out hallucination of Michel Foucault's theories on the nature of desire, madness, sexuality, freedom and incarceration. The author suggests that the extreme end of literary theory is to live it day-to-day separated from reality, an existence which eventually leads to madness and violence.

Anne Fleming

Death and Deconstruction. New York: St. Martin's Press, 1995. ISBN 0-312-13046-5. $19.95.

Fleming, a member of the Committee of the Byron Society and the *Byron Journal*, uses her literary knowledge of the Romantic period to satirize lit-crit factions. The London-based Coleridge and Other Romantic

Poets Society (RPS), which has been plagued by a series of nasty hoaxes, calls in Detective Chief Superintendent John Charter for undercover work during its upcoming conference at Norman Abbey. Before he can discover the hoaxer, two traditional English professor/critics are murdered. The prime suspects are the feminists and the "boa-Deconstructors," but as the plot unfolds, it appears that a missing Byron manuscript may be the murder motive.

Sandra M. Gilbert and Susan Gubar

Masterpiece Theatre: An Academic Melodrama. New Brunswick, NJ: Rutgers University Press, 1995. ISBN 0-8135-2182-3. $40.00. ISBN 0-8135- 2183-1. $15.95 pkb.

Set in the late 1980s, *Masterpiece Theatre* is a three-part literary drama about the abduction and attempted murder of a nameless Text, and the subsequent efforts of Jane Marple, a "very junior" assistant professor, to rescue it from villainous poststructuralists, Marxists, Eurocentrists, and various pop culture icons. The melodrama quotes liberally from the works of its large cast of real life characters (e.g., Camille Paglia, Julia Kristeva, Allan Bloom, Jacques Derrida, etc.) as it satirizes the culture wars. Gilbert and Gubar, professors, co-authors and co-editors of a number of works (*The Madwoman in the Attic*, *Norton Anthology of Literature by Women*, etc.), see themselves as part of academia's "excluded middle," set upon by extremists from both the Left and the Right. As Jane Marple notes at the end: "You were all to blame. Some of you wanted money, some political power, some professional advancement, some philosophical hegemony, some language games, some just general destruction" (p. 183).

Charles Grudin

Book: A Novel. New York: Random House, 1992. ISBN 0-679-41185-2. $19.00.

The plot of *Book*, which begins like a murder mystery, is only incidental and serves as a vehicle to satirize academia in general and the new wave of literary theories in particular. Adam Snell, a University of Washington English professor, suddenly vanishes along with all traces of his old-fashioned humanistic novel *Sovrana Sostrata*. Adam's trendier colleagues are suspect, but what they actually intend to kill or deconstruct, however, is the novel itself. The plot centers on a traditional chase–good guys versus bad guys–but in this case traditionalists are pitted against radical theorists. Stylistically parodying the self-conscious postmodern text, the novel slips in and out of several literary forms as well as from screenplay to epistolary novel to Cliff notes. Grudin intersperses the text with dustjacket blurbs, newspaper items, interviews, *Encyclopaedia Britannica* entries, diary excerpts, rebellious footnotes, a glossary, and harking all the way back to Andre Gide there is even the novelist commenting on his novel within the novel. In an odd way the novel is a tribute to the whole book which used to be read, loved and treasured.

Norman N. Holland

A Death in a Delphi Seminar: A Postmodern Mystery. Albany, NY: State
    University of New York Press, 1995. ISBN 0-7914-2599-1. $24.50.

In this postmodern take-off, prolific literary theorist Holland creates an academic mystery set on his former campus, SUNY Buffalo. During one "Delphi Seminar," in which graduate students are expected to present written and oral responses to assigned poems to their instructor (Professor Holland) and to each other, one student suddenly keels over dead, murdered by a poisoned thumbtack hidden under her chair. Holland and Lieutenant Norman ("Justin") Rhodes, a playwright in his off-hours, investigate, guided by Holland's own reader response theories and various narratives or texts: transcripts of police interviews, English department memos, newspaper accounts, and journal entries. Holland uses the novel to promote his own brand of reader response criticism, and it is no accident that the murder victim is an overweight, repulsive, blackmailing deconstructionist, who frequently disrupted the seminar to push her own pet literary theories.

D. J. H. Jones

Murder at the MLA: A Novel. Athens: University of Georgia Press, 1993.
    ISBN 0-8203-1502-8. $19.95.

An unusual serial killer has convened along with six thousand other attendees for the annual Modern Language Association convention. Hillbilly detective Board Dixon, baffled by the strange hothouse academics and their rites, recruits Nancy Cook, an untenured Yale professor, to give him a quick introductory course on the MLA. Since the crimes are as complicated as MLA politics and jargon, Cook remains throughout the novel with Dixon as a sort of tutor and literary helpmate. In the end they solve the murders by reading them as a contemporary text, complete with irony, contingency, randomness, and victim participation. Author Jones, whose pseudonymous identity is never revealed, more than likely represents a number of English faculty members. The book jacket blurb claims he/she has served as department chair at fourteen prestigious universities. The authors satirize the milieu of academic politics and literary criticism from insiders' perspectives, illuminating the gap between what passes for current literary scholarship and what is common sense.

David Lodge

Changing Places. New York: Penguin Books, 1979. ISBN 0-14-017098-7. $10.95.

Small World: An Academic Romance. New York: Penguin Books, 1996. ISBN 0-14-024486-7. $10.95.

Like Malcolm Bradbury, with whom he is often confused, David Lodge is a British university professor and literary critic whose novels often reflect his particular interest in critical theories of prose fiction. This interest is especially true of *Changing Places* (1975) and *Small World* (1985) where in the metafictional style of postmodernism, Lodge incorporates themes, styles, and theories of other authors. While ostensibly treating serious themes, these novels are also marvelously funny and draw upon their author's own experiences.

The primary focus in *Changing Places* is on two professors, the antithesis of one another, who temporarily exchange posts and, as a result, their values and personal lives. Modeled on Stanley Fish, Morris Zapp, an ugly American from Euphoria (Berkeley) U., is a vain, sarcastic, radical structuralist who replaces Philip Swallow, a mild, unpresuming traditionalist, at Rummidge University in England during the period of student unrest in the 1970s. Lodge tries out a number of narrative techniques in this work, and even has his characters consider the aesthetic problems he is facing.

The supposed death of the realistic novel which Swallow proclaims at the end of *Changing Places* may be the reason for the modification of *Small World* to the romance mode. Like Hawthorne, Lodge now claims for himself a "certain latitude" to suspend the circumstances normally attendant on human actions. Zapp and Swallow reappear but Peresse McGarrigle is the young, innocent hero who fits the pattern of Percival in the Arthurian legend. Peresse pursues his muse Angelica Pabst, a beautiful feminist graduate student, around the world from one literary conference to another. Like errant knights of old, academics from everywhere are constantly jetting in and out of literary conventions and seminars presenting their much-used-little-altered papers on Deconstruction, metaphor and metonymy, semiotics, morphemes and phonemes, etc. The virginal Peresse remains uncontaminated despite the randy, calculating, farcical scholars on their own quests for fame, trysts, jobs, and the UNESCO Chair of Literary Criticism, which carries an annual salary of $100,000 for doing nothing but some occasional thinking. Throughout the novel Lodge finds ample opportunities to take very funny swipes at reigning scholarly ideologies and present inside literary allusions, as well as jokes dealing with theoretical discourse.

Estelle Monbrun

Murder Chez Proust. Trans. by David Martyn. New York: Arcade Publishing, 1995. ISBN 1-55970-283-4. $19.95.

When the scheming head of the Proust Association is murdered at the home of the novelist's maternal aunt outside Chartres, various members of the literary elite become suspects: a graduate student who has just discovered 15 unpublished Proust notebooks which will make her reputation while destroying others; a well-known Proust scholar whose publications are plagiarized from his students' research; and a reclusive French critic whose celebrated fits of existential angst are really childish tantrums. Also suspect is an American Ivy League professor/critic on the prowl for a renowned "geneticist" to fill out his roster of literary theorists: "He had hired (and fired, when the need arose, in accordance with the rapidly changing fashions in literary criticism) a structuralist, a Marxist, a deconstructionist, and a feminist" (p. 65). The book is both a celebration of the works of Proust and a send-up of pseudo-Proustian criticism, academic careerists, and duplicitous literary critics.

When Monbrun (the pen name of French writer Elyane Dezon-Jones) first published her novel in France it caused quite a stir. Some readers associated the victim and the suspects with Proust scholars in New York and Paris. The real-life head of the Society of Friends of Marcel Proust, whose initials match those of the victim, was also not amused by her fictional counterpart. The author has denied that any of the novel's characters are based on real people, but the scandal was enough to propel the book on to France's best seller list.

Charles Palliser

Betrayals. New York: Ballantine Books, 1994. ISBN 0-345-36959-9. $23.00. ISBN 0-345-40435-1. $12.95 pbk.

Betrayals consists of ten interlocking stories, each a take-off on a different literary style, with one a parody of a literary interpretation of a text

("Lo(o)sing the Signifier: Silence, Wordlessness and Desire in Kipling's 'The Tongueless Boy' "). Much of the writing is deliberately awful and full of misspellings. The same characters reappear through the episodes, and often the same story is told several different ways, but all are interconnected by the theme of betrayal. Throughout the novel, the reader is invited to deconstruct the various narratives, which include an obituary, a fable, a book review, a trashy romantic novel, and a diary. One chapter, "The Medicine Man," satirizes European structuralism, describing the trials and tribulations of slimy world-renowned theorist Henri Galvanauskas, famous for never having published a single word under his own name. Galvanauskas' wife, disobeying her husband's orders that his words never be recorded, secretly tapes his lectures, revising them to ensure that "ambiguity, ellipsis, equivocations and even obfuscation were to be privileged over clarity, explicitness and logicality" (p. 85).

Ishmael Reed

Japanese by Spring. New York: Atheneum, 1993. ISBN 0-689-12072-9. $20.00.

A political tract as well as a darkly satiric campus novel, *Japanese by Spring* takes on theorists, feminists, male chauvinists, tenured radicals, and numerous ideologies, most notably political correctness. Benjamin (Chappie) Puttbutt, a junior African American English instructor at Oakland's fictitious Jack London University, hopes to gain tenure by becoming a sort of "intellectual houseboy," adopting various critical and cultural perspectives to serve his own self-interests. Believing that the Japanese are the next power brokers, he answers a newspaper ad to learn Japanese by spring. His timing is perfect. Shortly after losing his professorship to an overpaid Asian lesbian feminist poet/critic, Puttbutt finds himself appointed special assistant to the university president, his former language tutor, after the campus is taken over by an Asian investment firm. Puttbutt uses the opportunity to repay his old enemies: "Chappie was so happy that he was beside himself. He had sent a letter to the campus deconstructionists, informing them of their termination. The letters said you're fired. Those who believed that the words 'you're fired' meant exactly that could finish the semester. Those who felt that the words only referred to themselves would have to leave immediately" (p. 132). Reed, who also appears as a character in the novel, uses his comic narrative to attack academic follies and extremism as various campus factions–Old Miltonians, deconstructionists, feminist theorists, New Historicists, etc.–engage in vicious turf wars.

Cathleen Schine

Rameau's Niece: A Novel. New York: Ticknor & Fields, 1993. ISBN 0-395-65490-4. $19.95.

A combination marital comedy and send-up of academia and the post-modern cultural elite, *Rameau's Niece* satirizes the dogmatic absurdities of all academic theories, from Enlightenment rationality and empiricism to modern-day deconstruction. The main character, Margaret Nathan, famous for having written an academic tome on the wife of an obscure 18th-century French aristocrat adopted by feminists and deconstructionists (but never actually read) finds herself gradually seduced by a forgotten pornographic manuscript, "Rameau's Niece," she discovers in a library. The lascivious 18th-century treatise, plagiarized from Helvetius, Locke, Kant and Diderot's 1762 sketch, *Rameau's Nephew*, forces Nathan to "philosophically" investigate various theories as well as her life and marriage. Much of the book's humor comes from passages quoted from the imaginary manuscript and the oddball collection of literary sophisticates Nathan encounters: the French couple who spends their time deconstructing American paperback romance novels, calling them texts; the feminist critic who completes her dissertation on the deconstruction of restaurant menus; the female playwright who creates dramas featuring small groups of women sitting in large moving vehicles; the rising star of French theorists who concentrates on *The Federalist Papers*, etc.

Tom Stoppard

Arcadia. Boston: Faber and Faber, 1994. ISBN 0-571-16934-1. $8.95.

Stoppard has constructed *Arcadia* along two storylines: life at Sidley Park, the Coverly's country house in Derbyshire, in 1809 and life at present in the same house, where two very dissimilar academics are researching the Coverly family history among present day family descendants. Serious, staid landscape historian, critic and author Hannah Jones is writing a book about the hermitage and gardens at Sidley Park. Brash, sexist, pompous Bernard Nightingale, the other academic, is hungry for kudos in the academe and thus anxious to prove that Lord Bryon's hasty retreat from England was the result of a duel he could have fought at Sidley Park in 1809.

Similar to other fictional works discussed (*Possession: A Romance, Murder Chez Proust, Death and Deconstruction*), *Arcadia* involves disputes about the possession of literary manuscripts. Jones absurdly searches through early Nineteenth Century landscape records in order to prove that the entire Romantic movement was a sham. Nightingale, in turn, completely misinterprets book reviews, unpublished letters, and a signed collection of poems to gain fame and fortune. As the play shuttles back and forth between centuries and sets of characters, Stoppard parodies the competitive use of unpublished documents for critical one-upmanship and points out the follies of literary interpretation.

David Williamson

Dead White Males. Sydney: Currency Press, 1995. Available from Currency Press Ltd., P.O. Box 452, Paddington, NSW, 2021, Australia.

Dead White Males grew out of a literary conference attended by Williamson, an acclaimed Australian dramatist. After listening to a lecture on poststructuralism given by a young male academic to a roomful of writers, he noticed that no one in the room understood a word of the talk. When asked for a plain English translation, the lecturer told the writers that it was a difficult theory and that they shouldn't bother with it: "Just keep writing and we'll tell you what you've done." Angered by the tendency of academics to "treat writers as idiot savants who scribble away without knowing what they're doing," Williamson decided to write a social satire on literary theory.

This black comedy focuses on three main characters: Angela Judd, a young female literature student at New West University; Dr. Grain Swain, her lecturer in literary theory and the villain of the piece; and William Shakespeare, who is forced to defend his plays and literary viewpoint. The play is a contest between Shakespeare and French literary theory, a satire on theoreticist dogma, and a thoughtful treatise on the value of literature.

OTHER WORKS

Gates, Henry Louis. "Canon Confidential: A Sam Slade Caper." *New York Times*, March 25, 1990, sec. 7: 1.

In this spoof of hard-boiled detective fiction, detective Sam Slade is hired to check out the Western canon scam: "Seemed there was some kind of setup that determined which authors get on this A list of great literature. Payout was all perks, so far as I could make out. If you're on this list, they teach your work in school and write critical essays on you. Waldenbooks moved you from the Fiction section to the Literature section" (p. 1).

"Great Moments in Lit Crit." *Voice Literary Supplement*, no. 68, 1988:
9-12.

Drawn by S. B. Whitehead, this is a cartoon history of literary criticism
from the Stone Age to Deconstruction.

Sokal, Alan D. "Transgressing the Boundaries: Toward a Transformative
Hermeneutics of Quantum Gravity." *Social Text*, 46/47, vol. 14, nos.
1-2, Spring/Summer 1996: 217-252; "A Physicist Experiments with
Cultural Studies." *Lingua Franca*, May/June 1996: 62-64; "Mystery
Science Theater." *Lingua Franca*, July/August 1996: 55-64.

These three articles are included as examples of how anti-theory writing has permeated other disciplines. Tired of the arcane world of cultural
studies, Alan Sokal, a New York University physicist, submitted a parody
of literary and scientific jargon to *Social Text*, a scholarly cultural studies
journal. Passing the article off as a serious postmodern science critique,
Sokal's article proposed to develop a transformative hermeneutics of
quantum gravity (whatever that means) and included many elements common to critical theory: multiple parentheses, extensive footnotes, an elaborate bibliography, quotes from trendy theorists (e.g., Lacan, Derrida, Lyo-
tard, Irigaray), and meaningless abstractions (e.g., "counterhegemonic
narratives," "emancipatory mathematics," "morphogenetic fields"). After publication of this send-up, Sokal revealed in *Lingua Franca* that his
nonsensical article was a deliberate hoax. He contended that the accep-
tance of his "article exemplifies the intellectual arrogance of theory–postmodern literary theory, that is–carried to the logical extreme" (p. 63).
Social Text editors were shocked and appalled (although one is still not
convinced the article is a hoax), and Sokal's parody became a lively
discussion topic on the Internet, as well as elicting follow-up responses in
the next issue of *Lingua Franca*. As expected, literary critics and English
professors entered the fray. Stanley Fish, professor of English and execu-
tive director of Duke University Press, which publishes *Social Text*, de-
nounced the article as a "bad joke." On the other hand, Roger Kimball, a
long-time critic of theoretical jargon, lauded the bogus article.[4]

COLLECTION DEVELOPMENT SOURCES

The research methods and publication tools needed to track down and
acquire anti-theory fictional works vary widely. Monographs can be identified by searching individual and systemwide automated catalogs (e.g.,

MELVYL, RLIN, WorldCat, etc.). Journal articles on this growing sub-genre can be found by searching standard literary databases: the Arts and Humanities Citation Index, the Humanities Index, and/or the MLA Bibliography. Because these works are reactions to the explosion of critical theory that has occurred during the last two decades, current computerized versions of these files should suffice.

The challenge for researchers is identifying the subject headings used by catalogers or indexers. Although subject access has been added increasingly to online book records, the *Library of Congress Subject Headings* has long discouraged the addition of topical access to works of fiction. As a result, many theorifiction works lack subject heading access. At the same time, the headings used are diverse and inconsistent: Authors in Literature, Criticism–Humor, English Literature–History and Criticism–Fiction, Literature–Study and Teaching (Higher)–Fiction, Manuscripts–Fiction, Modern Language Association of America–Fiction, Universities and Colleges–Faculty–Fiction, etc. On occasion, individual works will be listed under broad subject categories (e.g., Criticism–Fiction); other times, the type of critical theory satirized will be singled out (e.g., Deconstruction–Fiction, Structuralism–Fiction, etc.). To complicate matters, online periodical indices will use some of the same headings but add additional subject terms as well: Critics in Literature, College Teachers in Literature, English Literature–Criticism, Teachers in Literature, etc.

Because much literary criticism comes from universities, it is also convenient for authors to make college campuses a setting for their works. For this reason, catalogers and indexers tend to lump anti-theory fictional works under the broad topical heading of campus fiction, but even this general subject varies from resource to resource. The *MLA Bibliography*, for instance, uses the descriptor Academic Fiction; the *Fiction Index*, Academics, Colleges, or Universities; the *Book Review Digest*, Fiction Themes–College Life or Fiction Themes–Teachers, etc. When consulting these library tools, researchers will not only have to check through a variety of terms but also work through extensive lists of titles.

Many critifiction works have received enormous critical and popular success. These books are nearly always reviewed in standard media sources: *Booklist*, *Kirkus*, *Library Journal* and *Publishers Weekly*. Also useful for reviews, but to a lesser extent, are the *London Review of Books* and the *Women's Review of Books*. A few authors, notably Malcolm Bradbury, David Lodge and Ishmael Reed, are known for their comic views of academics and literary theorists, but researchers can frequently spot new authors and works by regularly reviewing publisher announcements and catalogs, especially those issued by university presses.

It should be noted, though, that works in this subgenre may be viewed at two levels. On occasion, reviewers will comment on the comic plot or structure of these novels while overlooking theoretical approaches or attacks and missing inside jokes. There are so many critical schools of thought that it often takes someone familiar with a particular theory to pick theoretical references. *Textermination* and *Masterpiece Theatre*, for instance, are so layered with literary characters and critical schools that they require a very well-read researcher or scholar to pick out all the critics and critical theories satirized. Some periodicals, however, do have reviewers and/or contributors better able to spot this type of fiction. The following sources are particularly useful for contemporary fiction and drama: *Critical Quarterly, Critique, New York Times Book Review, Theatre Journal, TLS (Times Literary Supplement)*, and the *Yale Review*.

CONCLUSION

Critics have noted that articles in the *Publication of the Modern Language Association* (PMLA) are much funnier than any possible parody of them. Because MLA keeps pumping out obtuse theoretical articles for publication, fiction writers, many of them academics themselves, should have enough fodder to work with for decades to come. Academic libraries with strong literary theory collections should collect critifiction as a means of expanding their fiction collections, as well as balancing out their nonfiction critical collections. These satiric works provide an alternative perspective of literary theories not present in many of the impenetrable and narrowly focused texts published each year. Rarely do professional critics evaluate or examine their own theories. Clever, inventive works of critifiction perform a valuable service by demonstrating the excesses and flaws of literary theory. What makes these works delightful is the wonderful and hilarious way creative writers have skewered the whole critical theory industry.

REFERENCES

1. At the same time, there also has been a significant number of nonfiction anti-theory and theory debate works, including: James Atlas, *Battle of the Books: The Curriculum Debate in America* (New York: Norton, 1992); Bernard Bergonzi, *Exploding English: Criticism, Theory, Culture* (Oxford: Clarendon Press, 1990); William E. Cain, *The Crisis in Criticism: Theory, Literature and the Classroom* (Baltimore: John Hopkins University Press, 1984); John M. Ellis, *Against*

Deconstruction (Princeton, NJ: Princeton University Press, 1989); Howard Felperin, *Beyond Deconstruction: The Uses and Abuses of Literary Theory* (Oxford: Clarendon Press, 1985); Wendell V. Harris, *Literary Meaning: Reclaiming the Study of Literature* (Washington Sq., New York: New York University Press, 1995); Roger Kimball, *Tenured Radicals: How Politics Has Corrupted Our Higher Education* (New York: Harper and Row, 1990); Paul Lauter, *Canons and Contexts* (New York: Oxford University Press, 1991); W.J.T. Mitchell, ed., *Against Theory: Literary Studies and the New Pragmatism* (Chicago: University of Chicago Press, 1985); Peter Shaw, *Recovering American Literature* (Chicago, IL: I.R. Dee, 1994); Charles Sykes, *Profscam: Professors and the Demise of Higher Education* (New York: St. Martin's Press, 1988).

2. "Program," *PMLA: Publications of the Modern Language Association*, September 1994: 1162-1283, September 1995: 1179-1289.

3. Along with the growing collection of anti-theory nonfiction works, the MLA itself has been the subject of a number of critical articles, including Stephen Greenblatt, "The MLA on Trial," *Profession*, 1992: 39-41; Walter Kendrick, "Critics and Their Discontents," *New York Times*, 24 December 1995, Section 7: 12; Roger Kimball, "The Periphery vs. the Center: the MLA in Chicago," *New Criterion* vol. 9, no. 6 (February 1991): 8-17; Hilton Kramer and Roger Kimball, "Farewell to the MLA," *New Criterion*, February 1995: 5-16; George F. Will, "Literary Politics," *Newsweek*, April 22, 1991: 72.

4. Stanley Fish. "Professor Sokal's Bad Joke." *New York Times*, May 21 1996, sec. A.: 23; Roger Kimball. "A Painful Sting Within the Academic Hive," *Wall Street Journal*, May 29, 1996, sec. A: 18.

Index

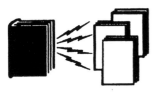

Haworth
DOCUMENT DELIVERY
SERVICE

This valuable service provides a single-article order form for any article from a Haworth journal.

- *Time Saving:* No running around from library to library to find a specific article.
- *Cost Effective:* All costs are kept down to a minimum.
- *Fast Delivery:* Choose from several options, including same-day FAX.
- *No Copyright Hassles:* You will be supplied by the original publisher.
- *Easy Payment:* Choose from several easy payment methods.

Open Accounts Welcome for ...
- Library Interlibrary Loan Departments
- Library Network/Consortia Wishing to Provide Single-Article Services
- Indexing/Abstracting Services with Single Article Provision Services
- Document Provision Brokers and Freelance Information Service Providers

---

MAIL or *FAX* THIS ENTIRE ORDER FORM TO:

Haworth Document Delivery Service
The Haworth Press, Inc.
10 Alice Street
Binghamton, NY 13904-1580

or **FAX:** 1-800-895-0582
or **CALL:** 1-800-342-9678
9am-5pm EST

PLEASE SEND ME PHOTOCOPIES OF THE FOLLOWING SINGLE ARTICLES:

1) Journal Title: _____

   Vol/Issue/Year: _____ Starting & Ending Pages: _____

   Article Title: _____

   _____

2) Journal Title: _____

   Vol/Issue/Year: _____ Starting & Ending Pages: _____

   Article Title: _____

   _____

3) Journal Title: _____

   Vol/Issue/Year: _____ Starting & Ending Pages: _____

   Article Title: _____

   _____

4) Journal Title: _____

   Vol/Issue/Year: _____ Starting & Ending Pages: _____

   Article Title: _____

   _____

(See other side for Costs and Payment Information)

COSTS: Please figure your cost to order quality copies of an article.

1. Set-up charge per article: $8.00
                    ($8.00 × number of separate articles)   _____

2. Photocopying charge for each article:

                           1-10 pages: $1.00   _____

                           11-19 pages: $3.00   _____

                           20-29 pages: $5.00   _____

                           30+ pages: $2.00/10 pages   _____

3. Flexicover (optional): $2.00/article   _____

4. Postage & Handling: US: $1.00 for the first article/

                        $.50 each additional article   _____

                        Federal Express: $25.00   _____

                        Outside US: $2.00 for first article/
                                $.50 each additional article_____

5. Same-day FAX service: $.35 per page   _____

GRAND TOTAL: _____

METHOD OF PAYMENT: (please check one)

❑ Check enclosed   ❑ Please ship and bill. PO # _____
                 (sorry we can ship and bill to bookstores only! All others must pre-pay)

❑ Charge to my credit card: ❑ Visa; ❑ MasterCard; ❑ Discover;
                    ❑ American Express;

Account Number: _____ Expiration date: _____

Signature: *X*_____

Name: _____ Institution: _____

Address: _____

       _____

City: _____ State:_____ Zip:_____

Phone Number: _____ FAX Number: _____

MAIL or *FAX* THIS ENTIRE ORDER FORM TO:

Haworth Document Delivery Service	**or FAX:** 1-800-895-0582
The Haworth Press, Inc.	**or CALL:** 1-800-342-9678
10 Alice Street	9am-5pm EST)
Binghamton, NY 13904-1580	